Henry Stevenson Washburn

The Vacant Chair And Other Poems

Henry Stevenson Washburn

The Vacant Chair And Other Poems

ISBN/EAN: 9783744704755

Printed in Europe, USA, Canada, Australia, Japan

Cover: Foto ©Thomas Meinert / pixelio.de

More available books at **www.hansebooks.com**

The Vacant Chair

AND

Other Poems.

BY

Henry Stevenson Washburn.

Silver, Burdett and Company,
New York . . . Boston . . . Chicago.

1895.

Copyright, 1895,
BY HENRY STEVENSON WASHBURN.

University Press:
JOHN WILSON AND SON, CAMBRIDGE, U.S.A.

These Verses, written in the leisure moments of a life devoted to business pursuits and matters of public concern, are published at the request of many friends, to whom they are affectionately dedicated by the author, as the shadows of fourscore years gather about his pathway.

CONTENTS.

Patriotic.

	PAGE
The Vacant Chair	13
Three Hundred and Ten	19
Ready for the War	21
The Deserted Camp of the Massachusetts Fifty-First	23
They are coming back daily, one by one	25
Keep green their Memories	27
God speed the Right	29
Massachusetts to South Carolina	30
Contrasts	32

Miscellaneous.

The Good Time coming	35
Fourth of July in Switzerland	38
John Bright at Seventy	40
A Day in June	42
The Bells of Vevay	44
The Rose	46
Sunset on Lake Winnipesaukee	47
The Marriage upon the Sidewalk	49
The Song and the Singer	53
The Boy Bathers	56

CONTENTS.

	PAGE
The East Wind	59
April	60
The hungry Students	61
Sunset on Lake Leman	67
Morning in the Isle of Wight	70
The Brook of my Boyhood	72
Among the Hills	75
Laura May	76
To the first Robin	78
The Lesson of the Morning	80
The Poet's Corner	82
To J. T. F.	85
A Sabbath in the Isle of Wight	86
Clerical Vestments	89
The Secret	93
Remembered Music	95
To a Forest Bird at Sunset	97
Kansas	98
Boston to Chicago	100
Burning of Chicago	102
Saturday Night	104
Only Waiting	106
The Pilgrim Fathers	109
Twilight	111
Boston Light in November	113
Upon the Sea	115
The last Robin	117
Song of the Harvest	119
The Week before Christmas	121
December	123
The Wayside Rest	124
Another Year	125
The Portrait Painter	126
To Samuel Francis Smith	127
Ode	129

	PAGE
Let every Heart rejoice and sing	131
Tremont Temple	133

Domestic.

Home	137
Eden	139
Boy and Maiden	142
The Cottage Bonnet	144
Early and Later Love	146
Our Old Homestead	148
Starting in Life	150
Thanksgiving Eve	152
The School-Boy's Vacation	154
The Trouble of the House	156
To N. at Thirty-two	159
Maria	161
Our Child	163
Our Household Pet	164
To A. at Twenty-one	166
A Sunbeam	168
Thy Name	170
Song of the Chip-bird	171
An Epistle from the Rhine	173
Our Cottage Home. No. 1	175
Our Cottage Home. No. 2	178
Meta	181
Mary	184
Shine and Shadow	186

Devotional.

Christ-like	189
One	190
The Glad Assurance	193

	PAGE
The Grave of the Dairyman's Daughter	194
She hath done what she could	197
The Still Small Voice	198
Storm on the Sabbath	199
Easter	201
In the Sanctuary	202
Winter Evening Hymn	204
The Village Church	205
Close of the Week	207
"Jesus Christ Himself"	209
"Trust in me"	211
The Pastor's Reception	212
Our Sanctuaries	214
The Rock of Ages	215
Zion	217
Dedicatory Hymn	219
Near to Port	221

Memorial.

The Great Mystery	225
The Smitten President	226
The Last Man at his Guns	228
Burial of Mrs. Judson	232
Henry Morton Dexter	234
The Harvest of Death	236
Samuel Lunt Caldwell	239

The Missionary's Bride.

The Missionary's Bride	243

PATRIOTIC.

THE VACANT CHAIR.

WE shall meet, but we shall miss him,
    There will be one vacant chair:
We shall linger to caress him,
When we breathe our evening prayer.

When a year ago we gathered,
    Joy was in his mild blue eye;
But a golden cord is severed,
    And our hopes in ruin lie.

At our fireside, sad and lonely,
    Often will the bosom swell
At remembrance of the story, —
    How our noble Willie fell;

How he strove to bear our banner
    Through the thickest of the fight,
And upheld our country's honor
    With the strength of manhood's might.

True, they tell us, wreaths of glory
    Evermore will deck his brow;
But this soothes the anguish, only,
    Sweeping o'er our heart-strings now.

Sleep to-day, O early fallen !
    In thy green and narrow bed :
Dirges from the pine and cypress
    Mingle with the tears we shed.

We shall meet, but we shall miss him,
    There will be one vacant chair ·
We shall linger to caress him,
    When we breathe our evening prayer.

WORCESTER, NOV. 16, 1861.

LIEUTENANT JOHN WILLIAM GROUT, the subject of "The Vacant Chair," was the only son of Jonathan and Mary Jane Grout, and was born in Worcester, Massachusetts, July 25th, 1843. His father was a successful business man, and the son enjoyed the excellent educational advantages given to the young in that enterprising city. He was a bright boy, and a favorite of his playmates, by whom he was familiarly known as Willie Grout. It soon was evident that he was by nature endowed with rare gifts, physically and mentally.

"Of medium stature and symmetrical proportions, erect carriage and remarkably fine and manly features, and with elastic vigor and the glow of health, he might have been selected as a model by an artist."

The photograph herewith given, which was taken just before his departure for the war, is an excellent likeness of his personal presence. He was a diligent student, and mastered easily subjects to which his attention was given; but he turned with special interest to history, in its relation to nations, and their conflicts one with another. He seemed to have been born for a military life; and inherited undoubtedly a love for the camp from his ancestors. "He was of the sixth generation from John of Sudbury, who was a grandson of an English Knight, and who distinguished himself for his heroism in leading his townsmen triumphantly against the assaults of the Indians in 1676, — for which he was rewarded with a Captaincy, then a substitute for Knighthood in England."

It was early a question what profession in life he should follow, — a matter which was not settled till he entered the Highland School in his native city, where in the Military Department his wishes were gratified. He joined the company of Cadets, and soon became its commander. Hardly had his ambibition been thus gratified, when the Civil War became the all-absorbing matter of interest to the people.

No one was quicker than he to see that his hour had come, and he desired at once to enter the army; but his parents withheld their consent for a while, chiefly on account of his youth, for he had barely attained the age when his country could legally claim his services. When however, they yielded to his importunity, his joy knew no bounds; and with all the ardor of his nature he began preparations for the service before him, such as sleeping on the floor to inure himself to the hardships of life in camp.

When the Massachusetts 15th Regiment was organized, he received the commission of second lieutenant of Company D, — an honor rarely bestowed upon so young a person. He was very popular in the regiment. His knowledge of military tactics was such that his services as a drill-master were in constant demand.

"He assured his friends, not with buoyant rashness, but with serious candor, that he had girded on his armor for all the emergencies of war, and for victory or death. He seemed to feel the solemnities as well as the responsibilites of his position, but never faltered in his purpose, or in the duties he was subsquently called to discharge.

"It was the fortune of the Massachusetts 15th Regiment to do the greatest execution, and suffer the greatest loss, in that disastrous conflict at Ball's Bluff, October 21, 1861."

The coolness, self-possession, and courage of Lieutenant Grout were noticed by his comrades with astonishment, and greatly stimulated the courage of others. When the day was lost, and they were forced to retreat to the river, he seemed to be utterly regardless of himself in his desire to have the wounded conveyed to the opposite shore. To his honor let it ever be remembered that he crossed the stream with a boat-load of the sufferers, and seeing them safely landed, returned to render like assistance to others; and continued so to do till he was obliged to plunge into the stream to save his own life. He had reached the middle of the river when he exclaimed to a comrade at his side, "Tell Company D I could have reached the shore, but I am shot, and must sink;" and as the waters closed over him, his spirit took its flight from the throes and conflicts of earth.

When his death was announced, Col. Devens with deep emotion said, "Dear little fellow; he came to me at the close of the battle and said, 'Colonel, can I do anything more for you?' and I replied, 'Nothing but take care of yourself.'"

For several weeks the Potomac held his body in its embrace, to be finally surrendered to loving hands, from whence it was tenderly borne to his native city for burial.

The heart of the old Commonwealth had never known a sadder day than when his remains, under the escort of the Highland Cadets, attended by the mayor and both branches of the city government, Col. Devens, and a large concourse of sympathizing citizens, were taken to the cemetery for interment.

Many tears were mingled with the volleys fired over the grave of the hero, who, at the early age of eighteen, fell a voluntary sacrifice upon the altar of his country.

THREE HUNDRED AND TEN!

When the battle at Ball's Bluff was announced, the mayor of Worcester despatched a messenger to the scene of action, with instructions to offer the Massachusetts Fifteenth Regiment, in behalf of the city, any assistance or succor they might require. He returned with this message: "Tell our friends at home that we want immediately *three hundred and ten men*, to fill the places of those killed and missing, and a blanket and pair of mittens for each of us. This is all we ask of them for the present."

LISTEN! wanted to-day, three hundred
    and ten
Of the strong and the brave of New
    England men:
They're wanted to fill a dread chasm that's made
In the gallant Fifteenth by the ball and the
    blade.
From the heart of the Commonwealth, steady
    and true,
The call To the Rescue! is sounded anew:
Ho! men of the anvil, ho! men of the plow,
Gird the armor on quickly; nay, tarry not now:
Ho! merchant and banker, ho! statesman and
    priest,
Ho! lawyer and client, ho! men at the feast,

To-day there are wanted three hundred and ten
Of the strong and the brave of New England
   men;
They are wanted to fill a dread chasm that's
   made
In the gallant Fifteenth by the ball and the blade.

We've a noble Republic to lose or to save, —
The boon that the blood of our ancestors gave;
A land that was flowing with honey and wine,
Till the cry of disunion polluted its shrine.
From the Heart of the Commonwealth, steady
   and true,
The call To the Rescue! is sounded anew:
By the love that we bear for our Puritan sires,
By our altars and temples, our bright winter
   fires, —
Our country, dear land of the free and the brave,
With the blessing of God, we are summoned to
   save.
Then on to the Rescue! Three hundred and ten
Of the strong and the brave of New England men,
You're wanted to fill the dread chasm that's
   made
In the gallant Fifteenth by the ball and the
   blade.

READY FOR THE WAR.

"I am going home to kiss my mother, and then I'm off for the War."
(Remark of a Volunteer.)

E stood beneath an autumn sky,
    A youth of proud and manly mien;
    The blast of war went wailing by,
And grief in many eyes was seen;
And pausing but a moment more,
    He ran to take one fond embrace,
Then sprang at duty's trumpet-call,
    To meet the foeman face to face.

And as he flew on eagle wing,
    His country's honor to defend,
I heard from lips all-quivering,
    His mother's prayer to Heaven ascend, —
"God shield, wherever duty leads,
    The darling of my heart to-night!
Upon Thy arm let him rely,
    The brave defender of the Right!"

Then from her couch bedewed with tears,
    Columbia, daughter of the skies,
Heard shouts transcending human fears,
    From hearts unawed, — " Arise, arise ! "
" No hand shall pluck a single star
    From that fair coronet of thine ;
The form his ruthless touch would mar
    Shall still in regal beauty shine ! "

The watchword leaped from out the waves
    That broke upon our rock-bound shores ;
It rang from Berkshire's granite caves,
    Where the proud bird of Freedom soars ;
From lake and stream, from hill and dell,
    One answering echo made reply,
" The Bay State knows her duty well, —
    Her sons will triumph — or will die ! "

And I am sure — since such as thine,
    Land of my Pilgrim sires and pride,
Their life-blood offer on thy shrine,
    And sternly battle side by side —
Our dear old flag will higher still,
    Wave proudly over land and sea ;
For those strong Saxon words, " We will,"
    Bear on to Victory the Free !

THE DESERTED CAMP OF THE MASSACHUSETTS FIFTY-FIRST.

NO sentinel paces his weary round,
　　Silent and lone is their camping-
　　　ground;
No roll-call at sunset, no drum-beat at morn,
No blast of the bugle, no peal of the horn!
They came when the harvest-moon, mellow and
　　mild,
Shone over the pathways of mother and child,
And the hunters' moon witnessed her tears as
　　they fell,
When her soldier boy whispered his last farewell.

I passed by the camp this brief dark day;
The snows of December upon it lay;
The murky skies like a leaden pall
Settled down drearily over all;
A silence oppressive pervaded the air,
And I tarried only a moment there, —
Only a moment, for the joy and the light
Of our homes and our altars have passed from
　　our sight.

Our noble boys of our brave Fifty-First,
Whom our hearts have cherished and hands have
 nurst,
They of the quick eye and fine manly brow, —
Tell us, O South Wind! where are they now?
And the South Wind answers, and this the reply:
"They're bearing the Stars and Stripes proudly
 on high;
Under the pines they are marching to-day,
Farther away — and still farther away!"

Father all-merciful, mighty and just,
Tenderly shelter our Fifty-First;
Nerve them for conflict with valor and might,
While they're defending the Truth and the
 Right;
Evermore shield them by night and by day,
Whilst marching away — and still farther away!

December 22, 1862.

THEY ARE COMING BACK DAILY, ONE BY ONE.

THEY are coming back daily, one by one ;
Their warfare is finished, their labor done :
'Mid the scenes of his childhood make room for the brave,
And give to our country's defender a grave !
With the signet of death on his fine manly brow,
Bear tenderly onward the young hero now ;
Let the drum beat a dirge while we lay him to rest,
And mingle our tears with the turf on his breast.
They are coming back daily, one by one ;
Their warfare is finished, their labor done.

They are coming back daily, but the quick eye is dim,
And motionless now the once vigorous limb,
The heart which beat only for country and fame
Is still, while we wreathe with fresh laurels his name.

We shall miss his glad shout when we welcome the dawn,
When the shadows of evening stretch over the lawn,
Oh, how we shall miss him, as year after year,
We come with our garlands to twine round his bier!
With the signet of death on his fine manly brow,
Bear tenderly onward the young hero now;
Let the drum beat a dirge while we lay him to rest,
And mingle our tears with the turf on his breast.
They are coming back daily, one by one;
Their warfare is finished, their labor done!

KEEP GREEN THEIR MEMORIES.

MEMORIAL HYMN.

KEEP green their memories, day by day.
    These pleasant paths with us they trod,
While prayer and praise beguiled the way
    To this dear temple of our God.

We knew not that the foeman's hand
    Was raised to strike the deadly blow;
That over all our happy land,
    So soon would break the wail of woe.

The heavens grew darker in that hour,
    When they, the noble and the brave,
Went forth in manhood's pride and power,
    And passed through victory to the grave

Such lives can never know decay ;
    New lustre gilds the martyr's name,
And greener, as time wears away,
    Is his immortal wreath of fame.

Then let our consecrated shrines
    Keep record of the early dead,
And treasure in undying lines
    The paths of glory they have led;

That lisping youth, and hoary age,
    While tears shall start and bosoms swell,
May read upon the marble page
    How Freedom's heroes fought and fell.

GOD SPEED THE RIGHT!

THE sun which rose through storm
 and strife
  Sets on a Land at peace;
For over all the bugle call
 Bids war and tumult cease;
And men who yesterday were seen
 Contending with their might,
With one accord let go the past,
 And shout, "God speed the Right!"

God speed the right! be this our prayer,
 Our earnest watch-word still,
As onward fair Columbia
 Her mission doth fulfil:
God speed the Right! O loyal heart,
 Trust now and evermore;
The bow of promise spans our land,
 From East to Western shore.

MASSACHUSETTS TO SOUTH CAROLINA.

On the sailing of the first steamer from Boston to Charleston at the close of the war.

PRAY tell us, brave pilot, what meaneth the signal
    The good ship unfurls as she leaps to the sea?
Where lieth the haven to which she is bearing
    The stars and the stripes, with the hopes of the Free?

" That flag to the world is a pledge of reunion,
    Of ties rudely sundered, reunited once more ;
Massachusetts to South Carolina sends greeting,
    As warmly and truly as ever before.

" Knew ye not, when the peal of the last gun of battle
    Died away from our valleys and hills, then arose
The Day-star of Peace, which o'er our broad acres,
    Its light on the nation benignantly throws?

"That star is our guide as to-day o'er the billows
The North to the South sends good wishes anew ;
With her prayer that our Union may be as enduring
As the pledge she now proffers is unstinted and true."

CONTRASTS.

E oft have seen when swept the tempest by,
The smiling rainbow in the weeping sky:

And we have seen when ocean's storms were o'er,
The placid ripple on the wave-washed shore.

MISCELLANEOUS.

IF, O cherished friend of mine,
You shall trace in any line
Aught herein which will impart
Strength and courage to your heart, —
Something making life more dear
As your footsteps linger here,—
Then not all in vain is flung
To the breeze the verse I 've sung ;
Doing better than I knew,
When I sang a strain for you.

THE GOOD TIME COMING.

> There's a good time coming, boys,
> A good time coming:
> We may not live to see the day,
> But earth shall glisten in the ray
> Of the good time coming;
> Wait a little longer.
> > CHARLES MACKAY.

THUS a bard of Britain prophesied;
 And his numbers, all aglow,
Passed o'er us like the breath of morn,
 Full many years ago.
And visions of the good time
 Came trooping into view,
And clothed the bright hereafter
 In tints of rainbow hue.

We dreamed of peace and plenty,
 Of the olive and the vine,
Of the reapers and the gleaners,
 Of the full corn and the wine;
We dreamed of shackles fallen,
 Of man erect and free,
Of golden cords of brotherhood,
 And anthems of the sea.

But while we waited, grimly,
    With iron heel and hand,
The War-God stalked triumphantly
    Through all our pleasant land;
And sobs and lamentations
    Went up from hill and plain,
For the manly hearts that quailed not,
    Upon our altars slain.

The years have come and vanished,
    But bitterness and strife
Still cast their baneful shadows
    O'er all that's dear in life.
Even now contention rageth,
    For borne on every breeze
Come tidings of the conflicts
    In lands beyond the seas.

The bard and prophet liveth,
    But what for human ken?
The good time's coming, is it?
    O weary watcher, when?
And countless heroes answer,
    Along the world's highways,
"O faint of heart, take courage!
    These are the better days.

THE GOOD TIME COMING.

" Hast thou not marked the progress
    Of knowledge among men? —
How mercy tempers justice,
    And th' sword yields to the pen?
How right o'er might prevaileth,
    How Peace her balm distils,
Whilst Ceres, smiling goddess,
    Her horn of plenty fills?
And fairer is the brightness,
    As Time his chart unrolls,
Of the light which comes to gladden
    All weary waiting souls.

" Yet never, yearning brother,
    Wilt thou perfection find ;
Some grain will be unwinnowed,
    Some gold be unrefined —
Some hearts will pine in sorrow,
    Some grope through doubt and fear ;
Oh, never canst thou realize
    The full fruition here.

" Still, over all forever,
    The star of hope will shine ;
After the frail and human
    Will come the life divine !"

FOURTH OF JULY IN SWITZER-LAND.

A STRANGER wandering through thy
    vales,
Land of the mountains wild and free !
Steps lighter as this July morn
    Breaks on his home beyond the sea ;

For whilst thy solitudes sublime
    Still lure him in his onward way,
His heart turns fondly back to where
    His country hails her natal day.

How like the whispers in a dream
    Come voices on the passing breeze ;
Dear messages of love and hope,
    From under the Atlantic seas.

And all day long as glide the hours,
    Those mystic cords of brotherhood,
Which link the old world with the new,
    Will thrill with greetings understood.

Brave land! our aims and hopes are one;
　The seed our fathers sowed we reap;
Upon thine everlasting hills,
　Doth Freedom bright her watch-fires keep.

Freedom! this is thy Jubilee!
　O mountain fastnesses which long
Have held the jewel in embrace,
　Join in the jubilate song.

And let the pæan onward roll,
　Till wars shall end and tumult cease;
And over every land, unfurled,
　Shall float thy banner, Prince of Peace!

JOHN BRIGHT AT SEVENTY.

WE send him greetings o'er the sea !
  Columbia's tried and steadfast
    friend ;
Most steadfast when her foes combined
  The laurels from her brow to rend.

His earnest eloquence is like
  The sturdy speech of Chatham's time,
When England's more than monarch hailed
  The glory of this Western clime, —

This goodly heritage of ours,
  Purged from th' oppressor's rod and sin,
Her ample gates wide open flung,
  For earth's worn millions to come in.

We have our mission, thou hast thine —
  O fatherland, to truth be true !
With the dead past we leave the old,
  And stretch our hands to clasp the new.

And we are glad so brave a heart,
  Reared at thine altars, sees the morn
Of liberty for all mankind,
  From out our night of suff'ring born.

JOHN BRIGHT AT SEVENTY.

His hand we hold in ours to-day,
   With blessings on his honored name,
While patriot hearts round all the world,
   Exult in his unsullied fame.

A DAY IN JUNE.

 FIELDS in June's fair verdure drest,
And vocal now with birds and bees!
A toiler from the world's highways
  I turn, with willing feet, to these,
  Inhaling here the morning breeze.

The air is moist with last night's rain,
  Through op'ning clouds the sun appears,
The robin, earliest of the train
  The plough-boy at his window hears,
  Repeats the song of other years.

I tread with lighter steps anew
  The pathways of my boyhood's morn;
The sky o'erhead is just as blue,
  And just as green the springing corn,
  And sweet the scent of thyme and thorn.

No care then rankled in my breast;
  No sorrow on my spirit fell;
The cool green sward my bare feet prest,
  The lowing herds they knew me well,
  And I, the daisy in the dell.

The squirrel had his hiding place,
  And I had mine beside the brook;
He gathered nuts from day to day,
    Whilst I a constant lesson took
    From him, and nature's wondrous book.

O fair green fields and summer skies!
  O visions of long time ago!
O well-remembered haunts, and chimes
    Which from perennial fountains flow!
    Glad voices from the vales below.

Here let me bathe my weary brow
  In this delicious air of day;
All laden as it cometh now
    With fragrance from the new-mown hay,
    The blackbird's and the robin's lay.

The busy world will not intrude,
  Nor Mammon his proud altar rear;
Alone, within this breezy wood,
    Where the Almighty doth appear,
    I'll pay my heart's deep homage here!

THE BELLS OF VEVAY.

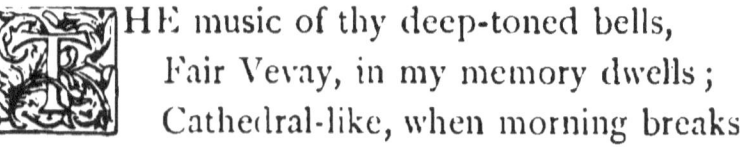HE music of thy deep-toned bells,
Fair Vevay, in my memory dwells;
Cathedral-like, when morning breaks
In beauty o'er thy crystal lakes;
Yet, liquid as a poet's rhymes,
The cadence of thy vesper chimes,
When sunset throws its crimson glow
On Dent-du-Midi's brow of snow,
When all released from toil and care,
They call the worshipper to prayer.

In old St. Martin's hallowed groves,
In fancy oft my spirit roves;
I pause beneath the chestnut trees,
And greet the cool, delicious breeze;
I gaze, till all my being thrills,
Upon the grand Savoyan hills;
And glimpses catch where Leman lies,
Serene beneath the summer skies —

When, lo! from out the old church-tower,
The bells proclaim the noon-tide hour;

To all the echoing heights around
Goes up the ever-gladsome sound;
The peasant, pausing 'mid his vines,
A while in welcome rest reclines,
And bird and bee, in bush and brake,
Seem to their hour of rest to take.

O Vevay bells! In joy and woe,
Thy message comes to high and low;
Thou hast a blessing for the bride
When standing by her lover's side;
A pæan for the true and brave;
A wail of sorrow for the grave;
A balm to soothe the troubled breast
When whispering to the weary rest;
For all, where joy or sorrow dwells,
Thou hast a message, Vevay bells!

THE ROSE.

HEN Adam first in Eden trod,
Fresh from the forming hand of God,
A rose, in vernal beauty drest,
Blushed sweetly on the earth's green breast;
Whilst Adam, filled with strange delight,
In wonder gazed upon the sight.

When lo! a form of virgin grace
Sprang forth to meet his warm embrace;
He plucked the rose so wond'rous fair,
And twined it in her golden hair,
Then stood enraptured by her side,
His blooming rose, and blushing bride.

With loving hands we still entwine,
The rose round woman's brow divine :
An emblem of that guileless hour
Ere sin had touched with blight the flower, —
An emblem, eloquent and pure,
Which shall the wrecks of Time endure.

SUNSET ON LAKE WINNIPESAUKEE.

HERE, when the long midsummer day
    declines,
And low winds murmur through the
    murmuring pines,
At that calm hour before may fall the dew,
When thought is busy and our words are few,
We climb the hills to see the setting sun
Proclaim afar another day is done.

Before us fair Winnipesaukee lies,
Reflecting Belknap towering in the skies;
Whilst Ossipee, twin brother of Red Hill,
The northern outlines of our vision fill:
Still nearer where the waning sun goes down,
The Domes of Sandwich all the landscape crown
And Moosilauk, the titan of the van,
A good-night's blessing sends to Cardigan.

High above all with wonder we behold
The sunset clouds their rainbow tints unfold;
Dissolving views, all blending into light,
A crown of glory on the brow of night;

The closing day another cycle fills,
As evening shadows glide among the hills.

Adown the lanes, still browsing, slowly go
The cows returning to the barns below,
Leaving perchance one wanderer in the field,
While they the nectar of the clover yield.
The cow-bell will her whereabouts disclose,
As after her th' impatient urchin goes;
Through bush and brake with temper unrestrained,
He drives her homeward; and, the barnyard gained,
He eats his supper with unquestioned zest,
Then falls away to boyhood's dreamless rest.

As shadows deepen, with his head erect,
Lingers awhile brave robin-red-breast yet;
The first to break the silence of the dawn,
And hail the coming of the rosy morn,
He well may be the last to say " Good-night,"
With heart as cheery as his song is bright.

Good-night, good-night ! O sufferer in the town,
I would the hills might send their blessing down;
That the pure tonic of this mountain air,
Might healing mingle with thy evening prayer:
Cheer up, poor heart ! whilst stars their vigils keep,
God ever giveth his beloved sleep.

THE MARRIAGE UPON THE SIDEWALK.

An incident of Boston in the olden time.

THE wind had changed; on Beacon Hill
　The crescent moon was shining still;
　The clock tolled out the hour of ten,
Just as the parson breathed "Amen,"
And with his hands crossed on his breast,
Welcomed another night of rest.

Soon underneath his window stood,
A gentle form of maidenhood,
Leaning upon his arm whose vow
Of love should be recorded now.

A rousing rap the parson woke,
And thus he from the window spoke:
"Who may you be, and why this call?"
"Doctor, the rain has ceased to fall,
The wind has changed, the moon shines bright,
I must be off to sea to-night;
Now let the deed be quickly done
Which shall proclaim that we are one."

The Doctor knew the captain's voice,
He knew the maiden of his choice,
Three times their banns were published well;
And as his words upon him fell,
He answered with his usual grace,
"Stand where you are, 't is just the place;
Now join together your right hands,
And you may start for foreign lands."

Then calmly on the midnight air.
He breathed for them a fervent prayer,
That God would their protector be
Whilst they were voyaging o'er the sea,

And bless, through all their coming life,
The twain who now were man and wife.

This done he to his blankets crept,
And as a worthy parson slept;
Whilst, standing in his manhood's pride,
The captain kissed his blushing bride;
And ere the morn broke o'er the bay,
His barque sped like a bird away.

A sweeter woman never graced
The path it o'er the ocean traced;
And whether winds blew high or low,
A gentle form passed to and fro,
A loving presence Heaven had sent,
To bless the ship where'er it went.

The voyage all o'er, how proudly now
The good ship tosses from her prow
The waters of their native bay!
Still beautiful before them lay
The port for which the spreading sail
Had wooed full long the passing gale;
Far they had wandered o'er the sea, —
Where two went out, there came back three;
And as the captain looked with joy
Upon the face of his bright boy,

He thought of something left undone,
When he and Mary were made one,
And quickly to the Doctor sped,
And standing with uncovered head,
Placed in his hands a marriage fee,
Due from that hour he went to sea —
How large a sailor's heart can be !
That time, when on the midnight air,
He breathed for them a fervent prayer,
When God gave him so good a wife,
To gladden all his coming life.

The moral to my tale is this, —
To hearts pledged for connubial bliss :
Start when the wind blows fair, nor wait
For morn to break before thy gate :
Life is a voyage, so spread thy sail
At once to catch the fav'ring gale ;
From street or church, from hut or hall,
Respond to Cupid's magic call ;
And howsoe'er thy lot may be,
Don't fail to pay the marriage fee.

THE SONG AND THE SINGER.

IN a quiet retreat near by the sea,
   In a dwelling humble and low,
A little girl stood by her mother's knee
And sweetly repeated a song for me,
   As rivulets sparkle and flow.

There was much to love in this little maid —
   Her heart was brimful of glee;
A delicate blush o'er her fair face strayed,
And sweet was the music her red lips made,
   As she sang this song for me.

I cannot tell you the words of the song
   She sang with her heart all aglow;
They were something about the shining throng,
Who wander the beautiful vales along,
   And th' bliss of Paradise know.

I thought as I listened unto her lay
   Such spirits to us are given,
To lure our feet whenever we stray,
Back into the straight and narrow way,
   The way that leadeth to Heaven.

A year passed on and I stood again
   In that dwelling humble and low;
'T was a July day, and the sturdy swain
Was busy cutting the ripened grain,
   And laying it row on row.

The crow of the cock and hum of the bee,
   And bobolink's magical tune,
And the distant chimes of the murm'ring sea,
Were just the same as they came to me,
   The summer before in June.

But that mother moved with a chastened air,
   And reverently bowed her head;
On her face were traces of recent care,
For a harp was silent which warbled there,
   And the light of her home had fled.

"And where is the child," I asked with surprise,
   "Whose heart was brimful of glee?"
And tenderly uttered were her replies:
"My darling in the graveyard lies,
   She 'll never come back to me."

Yet not a murmur escaped her lips, —
   "God giveth and taketh away;
The lamb which down in the meadow skips,
The bee which its fill of nectar sips,
   Have promise for only a day.

"But my dear one liveth forever more,
    My tears will not always flow;
I shall meet her again on the shining shore;
When this wearisome journey of life is o'er,
    I shall see her there, I know."

O mother bereaved! in thy faith I would share,
    As thy day, so is strength to thee given;
The Good Shepherd for her will tenderly care,
Thou wilt see thy lost darling glorified there,
    For of such is the Kingdom of Heaven.

THE BOY BATHERS.

In the summer of 1865 a number of boys, for the violation of an ordinance of the city of Boston prohibiting out-of-door bathing within its limits, were arrested and fined each two dollars. Being unable to pay the fine, they were imprisoned over night, when friends came to their relief and they were released. The event evoked sharp comment from the press, which led to the present system of free bathing-houses now so great a blessing, especially to the destitute classes.

TWELVE boys, one sultry summer day,
Had fun and frolic with the spray
Out in the waters of South Bay,

Upon our southern margin, where
The people breathe a purer air
Than the hot city has to spare.

The small waves played a merry chime,
While the boys had a jolly time,
And knew not that it was a crime.

And handsome brows which bore a stain
Grew fairer in the briny main,
And they all came out clean again.

That night those boys in prison lay
For this glad frolic with the spray
Upon this sultry summer day.

And the grim law imposed a fine
On those who made their faces shine
By plunging in the cleansing brine!

Oh, tell it not, my friends, in Gath,
That here poor boys can't take a bath,
But they incur the law's stern wrath;

That the great sea which laves our shores,
And health through every artery pours,
Keeping the plague-spot from our doors,

May not its healing powers dispense
For him who has less pounds than pence,
Lest thereby some should take offence.

Proud domes and palaces arise,
And towering spires salute the skies,
Filling the great world with surprise;

But nowhere has sweet Charity
Reared a fair temple by the sea,
Inscribing on its portals, FREE,

For all who will to come and go,
And here the pure waves welcome, ho !
The luxury of bliss below.

O brothers, freely God hath given
Pure water and the air of heaven,
To flow and blow from morn till even.

His hand, alike for great and small,
In ocean and the waterfall,
Hath stores enough for each and all ;

And let not metes nor bounds restrain
These blessings from the needy train
Who little have of this world's gain.

And let no act of ours oppress
The outcast and the fatherless, —
Those little ones whom Christ would bless ;

But choose we, rather, day by day,
Some load to lighten by the way,
Some heart to gladden while we may.

September 1, 1865.

THE EAST WIND.

THE east wind is coming, all moist with the spray,
And the odor of brine from the billows at play;
The hot day is ending, and this puff from the sea
Is like a fond kiss of my mother for me;
O day of midsummer! how gratefully now
This breeze from the ocean steals over my brow!

I remember that only two brief moons ago,
The east wind seemed coming from icebergs and snow,
So chill was its breath, and so frigid its mien,
While May flaunted gayly her banners of green.
But lo! with the smile of our beautiful June,
Came its wooing embrace with the bobolink's tune;
A herald of gladness passing graciously by,
To temper the heat of our fervid July.

O much abused east wind ! I will not again,
Methinks, of thy coming or presence complain ;
For lingering yet as a boon from the skies,
Thou 'rt blessing the couch where a sufferer lies ;
Giving strength to endure, and courage to bear,
His burden of pain, uncomplainingly, there ;
A respite from anguish, whilst soothingly now
Thy breath from the ocean is fanning his brow.

APRIL.

The crocus rears its purple crest,
    Beside the wasting banks of snow ;
Whilst merrily the wayside rills
    Unfettered through the meadows flow.

Come forth with me ! the winsome smile
    Of this capricious April day
Will wake to fairy life the buds,
    To blossom on the brow of May.

THE HUNGRY STUDENTS.

The following incident occurred when Boston was a small city, and there was no communication between it and its suburbs, except by omnibus or stage once or twice a day.

Lunch or eating houses were unknown; and delegates to religious gatherings were entertained at private residences, to which on this occasion the parties here introduced were unintentionally not invited.

EAR where the shaft on Bunker Hill
   Points upward to the sky,
The hosts of Zion gathered once,
   To praise the Lord most High.

They came from hall and hamlet round,
   And cast their off'rings down,
And hallowed was the scene that day,
   In that historic town.

Two manly men, young Levites they,
   From Newton joined the throng,
And bowed with older prophets there,
   In prayer and sacred song.

But little to sustain the flesh
    They 'd eaten through the day,
When with the setting of the sun
    They homeward took their way.

From many unassuming homes
    The evening fire-lights gleamed,
And happy groups round supper-boards,
    To them in Eden seemed.

And musing as they passed along
    Where Harvard's shadows fell,
They fancied that her many sons
    Could some good stories tell, —

Of hungry students feasting long
    O'er well-picked chicken-bones,
While humor made the old halls ring,
    In no unmeasured tones.

There little was in this long walk
    Their spirits to beguile,
With hunger gnawing at their breasts,
    And every rod a mile.

Yet on they went till all the stars
    Of night began to shine,
And Watertown at last was reached,
    As bells rang out for nine.

Then with unbounded joy they hailed
    The ever-open door
Of Deacon Coolidge, who had been
    Their steadfast friend before.

The Deacon heard the pleasant tale
    Of all they saw that day,
How blessings fell upon the men
    Who met to praise and pray:

Presuming that their mortal part
    Had been as richly fed,
He took a candle quietly,
    And led them off to bed.

Too modest they to give a hint,
    Though sore by hunger prest,
And supperless, these stalwart men
    Lay down that night to rest.

But ere that sleep, dear balmy sleep,
    Shut out from human ken
All knowledge of themselves, they thought
    Of other hungry men —

How it were well the flesh at times
  To crucify and slay,
That saints and sages fasted long
  When they retired to pray;

And though the cup were bitter, still
  It would be for the best;
It were enough the Master gave
  To His belovèd rest.

Then praying that the Lord till morn
  Would them in safety keep,
These famished students gradually
  Fell off in troubled sleep.

———

Not long had they been slumbering,
  When dreams stole o'er the brain
Of Brother Neale, and lo! he dreamed
  That he was once again

Beside a table spread with all
  A hungry man could eat;
And blessing he was asked to crave,
  Upon the bread and meat.

So dreaming on, with hands upraised,
    Unconsciously he said,
" Dear Father, bless this bounty now
    Before Thy servants spread."

His voice awoke his Brother Swaim,
    Who, starting as if hit,
Sprang up exclaiming, " Brother Neale,
    Good gracious! where is it?"

Alas, alas! 't was all a dream,
    No feast before them lay;
And wearily dragged on the hours
    Until the break of day.

And not before the tardy sun
    Had risen o'er the hill,
Did they at the good Deacon's board,
    Their hungry stomachs fill.

Then Newton, school for prophets still,
    They reached with easy pace,
Where students still have appetites,
    In keeping with the place.

Thenceforward as Time rolled along,
    And visions came and went,
These prophets of the Lord recalled
    That night of hunger spent;

And thought it was like much they oft
    Had seen along their way;
How life had passed just like a dream,
    While they were growing gray;

That often, when the day was dark,
    And they had prayed for bread,
The light appeared, and Heavenly Love
    A feast before them spread.

SUNSET ON LAKE LEMAN.

LEMAN ! famed in song and story,
    Let me float upon thy breast,
    Like a bird with folded pinions,
At this sunset hour of rest ;
And between the lapsing pauses
    Of the half-suspended oar,
Let me listen to the music
    Wafted from the vine-clad shore :

Softer still, O sturdy boatman!
   Lighter dip the yielding oar;
While I listen, listen, listen,
   To the music from the shore!

Through the purple mists of evening,
   Grandly rise the mighty hills,
From whose hidden depths and fountains
   Freely gush the crystal rills;
Even now I fancy, mingling
   With the music from the shore,
I can hear the laughing waters
   When the boatman rests his oar:
      Softer still, O sturdy boatman!
         Lighter dip the yielding oar;
      While I listen, listen, listen,
         To the music from the shore!

All too brief, O shrine of beauty!
   Are these golden hours for me;
All too soon will leagues of distance
   Stretch between my home and thee:
Yet my spirit here will linger,
   And my little boat will glide,
Often at the hour of sunset,
   O'er thy blue unruffled tide:

Softer still, O sturdy boatman !
Lighter dip the yielding oar,
While I listen, listen, listen,
To the music from the shore !

VEVAY, SWITZERLAND.

MORNING IN THE ISLE OF WIGHT.

OW fair, dear Annie, is the smile
Of morning, on this sea-girt isle !
Come, leave thy books and cares to-
day,
And hie thee to the downs away, —
The breezy downs, where, in the dells,
The heather swings its purple bells ;
The gray old downs, which rise and frown,
Like sentinels above the town ;
These be our chosen haunts to-day,
As pass the summer hours away.

How grandly o'er the curling tide
The ships of every nation glide !
Through England's mighty channel bent,
With cargoes from the Continent ;
With wealth from India and Peru,
Stores of the old world and the new ;
Their white wings coying with the breeze, —
Were ever fairer seas than these?

MORNING IN THE ISLE OF WIGHT.

Did ever skies of deeper blue
Exhale the drops of crystal dew?
Did ever skylark sweeter sing,
Borne upward on exultant wing?
Say, Annie, in the wide world round,
Where can you find more fairy ground, —
Where morning's dawn and evening's close
Bring to the weary more repose?
What spot on all the earth more bright
Than England's famous Isle of Wight?

VENTOR, ISLE OF WIGHT.

THE BROOK OF MY BOYHOOD.

THERE is a brook, a merry brook,
    Whose waters glide away,
And creep into each tiny nook,
    Like a little child at play.

It runneth by my grandsire's door
    The same as when a child
'Twas my delight to hear it pour,
    Its music on the wild.

The passing stranger may not heed
    This modest little rill,
Which wanders through the verdant mead
    Its pleasant journey still:

But unto me, O stream! a voice
    Hast thou of bygone years;
I cannot see thee but rejoice,
    I cannot but with tears.

'T is not because the hills and vales
  Through which thy pathway lies
Are fairer than the hills and dales
  Beneath a thousand skies, —

Nor yet because thy waters leap,
  So joyously and free;
No, not alone for these I keep
  This early love for thee.

'T is for the past that thou canst stir
  Fond memories at thy will,
For halcyon days that I prefer
  Thy sparkling waters still.

Still mirrored on thy breast I trace
  Bright visions flitting by;
I see a boy with sun-browned face,
  And laughter in his eye,

Who cares not, in his fair young prime,
  With spirits all aglow,
That there may be a coming time,
  When tears, alas! will flow.

Oh memory! priceless boon to all!
  When of thee we 're denied,
How hard the struggle to recall,
  Who lived, who loved, who died.

Then thanks to thee, thou little stream,
  For the record thou dost bear
Of scenes which linger like a dream
  In my remembrance there.

A toiler from a world of strife,
  I fondly turn to thee ;
Full soon must end this checkered life,
  Bear record then of me.

AMONG THE HILLS.

HEN Morn the gates of Day unlocks,
We hear the crowing of the cocks ;
And from the maple groves below,
The cawing of the hungry crow ;
And later, from the clover dells,
The tinkling of the cattle bells ;
And later still, the hum of bees ;
And whisp'rings in the forest trees ;
With now and then from field and fold,
Glad voices as the day grows old.

Among the hills ! away from care,
The tonic of this mountain air
Comes as a benediction now ;
O restless heart and throbbing brow !
How kindly Nature sheds her balm,
Amid this universal calm !
How soothingly, upon her breast,
She gives her weary children *rest !*

LAURA MAY.

BESIDE a pleasant waterfall,
   In an unfrequented way,
   A merry little maiden lives,
Whose name is Laura May.
Her father is a farmer,
   And toils hard and long,
But ever with a happy heart
   And a bosom light with song.

But little of this busy world
   This fairy child hath seen ;
Her playmates in the village live,
   Her sports are on the green ;
And fragrant as the wild flowers
   That bloom along the way,
Are the unobtrusive virtues
   Of little Laura May.

When first I saw her sitting
   Beside her father's door,
I thought so much of innocence
   I had not seen before ;

Upon her neck of snowy white
    Her auburn tresses lay —
Oh very fair and beautiful,
    Is little Laura May!

And thus in quiet places
    By waterfall and glen,
In paths but seldom trodden
    By the restless feet of men,
The fairest flowers blossom,
    The coolest fountains play,
And all unseen, unnoticed, lives
    Some charming Laura May.

Go thou whose heart is weary
    With the burdens and the strife,
With the longings and the cravings,
    The jealousies of life —
Go take thy staff and travel
    Upon the world's highway,
And thou shalt find in many a cot,
    The soul of Laura May!

TO THE FIRST ROBIN.

 WELCOME warm awaits thee,
    Bright herald of the spring;
    Thy voice of winning sweetness
  Has still its merry ring.
The winter days are over,
And buttercups and clover
Will gladden all the way
In which thy feet may stray,
    Whilst thou singest, singest
Thy old familiar song,
As the seasons roll along,
    Robin, Robin!

Thou hast tarried long and late,
A questioner of fate,
Feeling cautiously thy way,
In thy coming day by day.
Now take a crumb or two,
And cheer thee up anew;
The pastures, bleak and sere,
In beauty will appear;

And the roaring northern blast,
Be a memory of the past,
   Whilst thou singest, singest
Thy old familiar song,
As the seasons roll along,
      Robin, Robin!

Oh, thou 'lt be surpassing sweet,
With thy nimble little feet
Tripping lightly o'er the lawn
At the breaking of the dawn,
   And "Good-morning, summer's coming."
Not a harbinger of spring,
However sweetly he may sing,
   Can sing as thou singest, singest
Thy old familiar song.
As the seasons roll along,
      Robin, Robin!

THE LESSON OF THE MORNING.

Y hand is on my garden gate,
    The dew-drops tremble on the thorn,
    The forest birds are all elate,
And carol to the rosy morn ;
Ho ! forest bird and rising sun !
    As roll the mists of night away,
For me, who long the race hath run,
    What message have you brought to-day?

I slept, for darkness deepened round ;
    I woke, for light illum'd my room ;
And silence, which had reigned profound,
    Passed with the darkness and the gloom.
The miracle of life again
    My op'ning eyes with joy behold,
As voices now of earnest men
    Are coming up from field and fold.
Ho ! forest bird and rising sun !
    What message have you brought for me?
I, who so long the race hath run,
    Would fain the goal before me see.

ANSWER.

"There comes a night, how dark and long
　Is not revealed to mortal men ;
Yet pilgrim, let thy heart be strong,
　The day will follow night again.
So take thy staff and travel on,
　Through what of joy or woe betide ;
Thou wilt a priceless boon have won,
　If Faith go with thee side by side."

THE POET'S CORNER.

 N an old-fashioned building,
    On a very busy street,
    A poet [1] hale and hearty
Has a coveted retreat,
Where behind a green baize curtain
    He finds relief from care,
And has for many callers
    A cordial welcome there.

[1] James T. Fields. His business life was passed in the Old Corner Bookstore, and his " coveted retreat " was on the School Street side of the building.

Around this corner gather
    The toilers of the pen, —
The foremost and the bravest
    Of our wise and witty men;
For much they love the poet,
    And they like his cosy seat;
'Tis a fountain in the desert,
    Where congenial spirits meet.

I sometimes draw the curtain,
    But step at once aside,
For Emerson and Longfellow
    The morning hour divide;
Or Whittier, the beloved,
    As brave as he is true,
With Lowell, Holmes, and Hawthorne
    Old fellowships renew.

Then with books and friends I linger,
    And loiter till my turn,
And fumble over volumes
    That with words of beauty burn,
Till these master-minds have entered,
    And passed along their way,
When we have a talk together,
    In the quiet of the day.

I think that time is dealing
　Very gently with my friend;
Not a wrinkle with the crimson
　Has yet begun to blend;
Not a gray lock with the auburn
　Upon his forehead plays,
And his step is still as certain
　As in our younger days.

Heaven save that ancient building
　From the innovator's hand!
As a landmark of our fathers
　Let this corner bookstore stand:
For cherished memories lure us
　As we wander down the street,
To the poet in his corner,
　To this scholar's calm retreat.

1855

TO J. T. F.

ACCEPT, I pray, this wayside flower,
    It blossomed by a mountain rill;
    I plucked it at that early hour
When birds the brakes with music fill.

I thought it only bloomed for me;
    It answered, " Nay, for thee, for thee;"
And so I 've brought it all the way,
    To cheer thy heart, friend Fields, to-day.

A SABBATH IN THE ISLE OF WIGHT.

To Mrs. A. M.

DEAR friend, and will it be so soon
As after one more summer moon,
Your busy feet will roam no more,
The hills and vales of England o'er?
That scenes which charm the eye and ear,
Will fade away and disappear,
And many leagues of raging sea,
Will roll between these shores and thee?

Well, distance never may efface
The memories of the paths we trace;
And often in your northern home,
When the November days shall come, —
When seated at your open fire,
As the last beams of day retire, —
You will recall this Sabbath bright,
You spent upon the Isle of Wight, —

This day of more than regal bloom,
Unsullied by a tinge of gloom;
Pure type, to weary mortals given,
Of the sabbatic rest of heaven.

Yes, these fair fields, this sky so blue,
These wayside flowers of every hue.
This mighty sweep of sea and shore,
The cliffs the breakers thunder o'er —
Yon dear Bon Church, close nestled there,
'Mid ivy bowers, sweet place for prayer —

The dead who in its shadows sleep,
Lulled by the voices of the deep, —
These, at your call will come and go,
When at your casement beats the snow.

And loved ones oft will listen well,
To the fine story you can tell,
How, when your locks were turning gray,
You travelled far from home away,
And lingered long by castle walls,
And music heard in waterfalls,
And realized in mount and streams,
The visions of your early dreams.

Ventor, August, 1877.

CLERICAL VESTMENTS.

An incident in the lives of Drs. Thomas Baldwin and Daniel Sharp, clergymen, eminent in Boston between the years 1790 and 1853, for thirty-five, and forty-one years respectively.

AT the old church in Baldwin Place,
 Where long good-will abounded,
A trifling matter one fair morn
 Was seriously propounded.

'Twas when before its altar bowed
 That man whose name is graven,
On many hearts as he who lured
 The weary soul to heaven.

He moved serene in gown and bands
 His flock the shepherd leading;
And tenderly for high or low,
 Alike their wishes heeding.

It chanced an English preacher once —
 A youth of modest bearing,
A Sabbath passed with Dr. B.,
 His pulpit labor sharing.

The elder in the morning traced
    The narrow way to glory,
The young man in the afternoon,
    Repeated Calvary's story.

Next day they passed a quiet hour
    In social conversation,
And talked of men whose lives were marked
    By earnest consecration, —

How prophets and apostles preached,
    How eyes with rapture glistened
When Jesus spake the words of life,
    To multitudes who listened.

" And do you think in gown and bands
    The preacher then appeared ? "
Asked Mr. Sharp, who never had
    The gown and bands revered.

" I liked your sermon very much,"
    Continued Mr. S.
" But had you preached without that robe,
    I had not liked it less."

" I 'm sorry that my old silk gown,"
    Retorted Doctor B.,
" Was yesterday a stumbling-block,
    Between my Lord and thee ;

"But, Brother Sharp, last evening, when
  The Sabbath feasts were ending,
Old Sister Lee came up beneath
  Her fourscore winters bending,

"And in her simple way declared,
  How much she liked your sermon,
That to her thirsty soul your words,
  Were as the dews of Hermon :

"And yet she said, '*I hate a fop*,'
  As if some pain beset her,
'But for his ruffled-bosom shirt,
  I should have liked him better.'"

The young man smiled, he saw the point,
  Too plain for doubt or guessing ;
And bowed before his senior there,
  And knew he had his blessing.

'T was just before he passed away,
  Ere yet was loosed the cable,
That Doctor Sharp this story told,
  One evening at my table.

As mellow as an autumn sky,
  As ripe as golden grain,
He seemed that night to me and mine,
  As he rehearsed again —

That record of a nobler life,
   Its failures and successes,
His faith in that sweet charity
   Which purifies and blesses —

Which scorns to cross and criticise
   What is the merest trifle,
Well knowing that the nobler part,
   We thereby mar and stifle.

And so I muse — if we could " see
   Ourselves as others see us,"
The beam which often dims our eyes
   Would not so oft mislead us.

THE SECRET.

 LITTLE brook went singing on
    Where M. and I were straying;
It held a secret in its breast,
    Yet evermore was saying,
        "*Some* day."

The days sped on, and still the brook,
    Through all our smiles and sighing,
The secret kept, whilst merrily
    The selfsame words replying,
        "*Some* day."

Somehow a robin chanced to guess
    The secret we were keeping,
And told it to his gentle mate,
    The very words repeating,
        "*Some* day."

But brook and bird, whilst seemingly
    Our earnest wishes heeding,
Could not refrain from whispering
    Each rosy morn succeeding,
        "*Some* day."

Dear little stream, there came a time
   Of very sweet revealing,
When we no longer wished nor cared
   For any more concealing,
      One day.

We rank it with the golden hours
   Which blessed our life's young morning;
And see fulfilled at eventide,
   The promise of its dawning,
      That day!

REMEMBERED MUSIC.

THE preacher had his sermon preached,
    And prayer befitting marked its close,
When, ling'ring yet where prayer was
    made,
    The preacher and the people rose.
The choir sang sweetly an old hymn,
    Which most before had never known;
But there were some whose eyes were dim,
    To whom it spake of years long flown,
When with a low and reverent air,
    They trod the hallowed aisles of prayer.

The young were moved and wondered why
    They had not heard those strains before;
The old man wept and seemed again
    To live his very childhood o'er.
As quickly, from the treasured past,
    Came visions of the olden time,
When his dear father worshipped God,
    Whilst swaying to the music's chime,

And by his side they sat who shared
  The sunshine of his early days;
What other could he do than weep,
  To hear once more these good old lays?

Oh, art may charm, and newer strains
  May better please the youthful breast,
But unto him whose locks are gray,
  The oldest music is the best.
And so I felt, as died away
  Those strains within that place of prayer,
That heaven to some will sweeter be
  If " Dundee " is remembered there.

TO A FOREST BIRD AT SUNSET.

'T is night on the mountains — yet, beau
 tiful bird,
Thou art singing a song which the
 forest has stirred ;
The mild mellow evening bends down from above,
As its dim aisles re-echo thy ditties of love, —
Deliciously sweet, and as lute-like and clear
As if borne to the earth from some holier sphere!

I listen and wait, as still one more refrain
Passes by on the breath of the evening again, —
Now rising, now falling, now dying away,
Like the chimes of the ocean, or breezes at play ;
A good-night for all, ere thou fallest asleep,
And stars o'er the hamlets their lone vigils keep.

I have left the thronged marts and turmoil of men,
For the quiet which reigns in this wild-wood and
 glen ;
And I fain would believe thy song is for me,
Thou magical ranger o'er forest and lea.
The scenes of this twilight may vanish away,
But never, no, never, the charm of thy lay.

KANSAS.

JUNE breathed her benedictions when I
stood
Where thy green summits, Lawrence,
overlook
City and hamlet, vale and winding stream,
And prairie vast, as fair and beautiful,
In all their virgin freshness, as a bride
Decked for her nuptials. It was even-tide.
The sun, breaking through clouds which just before
Had dropped their rain, whilst sharp the lightnings flashed
And the dread thunder rolled, serenely now
Upon a bed of crimson sank to rest.
Oh, never fairer visions blessed mine eyes!
Far in the distance waved the rip'ning wheat,
And the young corn, covering broad acres,
Tossed its green blades exultingly. Near by,
In garden bowers, the clustering grape
And golden nectarine sure promise gave
Of autumn fruitage and of harvest-cheer.

The cattle, sleek and noble, half concealed
Amid the blooming clover, flecked the glades;
Whilst merrily the birds their roundelay
Poured forth, and every tree, and wayside hedge
Sparkled with rain-drops in the setting sun.

And as I mused at this sweet evening time,
I seemed to hear that voice which Adam heard
At the cool hour of day, saying: *"Be still,
And know that I am God!* But yesterday,
From this fair summit thou hadst seen ruin
And death; on every side war's dread alarm;
The torch of treason, and a town in flames!
Yet, as the tempest which an hour ago
Swept o'er the sky, scattering its thunderbolts,
And pouring out the vials of its wrath,
Now flies apace, its awful blackness spanned
By the glad bow of promise, leaving earth
More beautiful than ever, — so Kansas,
Green garden of the continent, comes forth
From the fierce furnace of her sufferings,
In purer vestments clad, since clouds that hung
Over her fair domain have passed away,
And peace and plenty gladden all the land."

BOSTON TO CHICAGO.

 GREETING and blessing, Chicago!
    A right hearty shake of the hand;
    You are sending us many car-loads
  Of the needful things of the land;
And we in turn are remitting
  Our thousands of silver and gold;
Let the bond of our friendship forever
  Be strong as our Union is old.

We 're piercing the sides of the mountains,
  We are sweeping o'er valley and plain,
To tap the springs at their fountains
  And gather the golden grain;
And our New England pluck, remember,
  Now our hand has hold of the plough,
Will not suffer its grasp to surrender
  Till we 're nearer together than now.

We have given you something, Chicago,
  More precious than silver or gold;
Treasures dearer than gems of the mountains
  Your loving embraces enfold:

You 've won to your shrines and your altars,
  At Friendship's and Fortune's behest,
Our sons, and our beautiful daughters,
  O magical Queen of the West!

God give thee good speed in thy mission,
  To thy giant young energies play;
The wealth of the valleys compressing
  In the garners you 're filling to-day.
The hungry of earth will require it,
  The Great Father's bountiful store;
Oh, scatter it widely, and send it
  To the dwellers on every shore.

And the song of praise and thanksgiving
  From millions far over the sea,
Will swell to an anthem of gladness
  As its echoes come backward to thee.
And so long as the earth buds and blossoms,
  And the reaper still gathers the grain,
And our banner of stars floats unsullied,
  May this bond of our Union remain.

1867.

BURNING OF CHICAGO.

 WALKED among thy palaces,
    A few brief moons ago ;
    The prairie blossomed as the rose,
The lake lay calm below ;
Of all the land thou seemed most blessed,
O fair Queen City of the West !

I could not know so great a woe
    For thee was kept in store, —
That I should look with pride upon
    Thy matchless form no more ;
That the fire-demon, sweeping past,
Would hurl on thee his dreadful blast.

Great city of unvanquished souls !
    Our hearts will turn to thee ;
Thy sorrow chastens all our joy,
    It leaps from sea to sea ;
From hut and hall I hear one prayer,
" God let us in thy suffering share."

Oh, mighty cord of brotherhood !
   Amid earth's wrongs and strife,
How grandly breaks upon our view
   This golden side of life ;
The nations read in thy great light,
Chicago ! glorious truths to-night !

Then take our blessing and our love,
   The dear old love of yore ;
We know that thou wilt rise again,
   As stately as before ;
Where now thy ruined columns stand,
We 'll clasp again thy strong right hand.

1872.

SATURDAY NIGHT.

HO, brothers on life's length'ning way;
    To-night, as in the golden West
    The sun goes down, I hear a voice
To our tired spirits whispering, " Rest ! "

Shut off the water from the wheel,
    And let the busy mill be still ;
Leave Care and Traffic with their scores
    Of gain and loss, in good and ill.

Poor pilgrims, longing evermore,
    We've bowed at many a tempting shrine :
Too far astray, our hearts to-night
    Cry out for something more divine.

What were our life, if all between
    Its crowded days of joy and grief,
The Sabbath did not intervene
    With its sweet breathings of relief?

Then hail, O weary heart, with me,
 This hour of rest from labor given;
The antepast of Peace which reigns
 Within the op'ning gates of heaven.

From the celestial heights we gain
 In this surcease of care and strife,
How breaks upon our view that Land
 Whose boundaries are Eternal Life!

ONLY WAITING.

BESIDE a river where forest and field,
    Slope gracefully down to the shore,
A man and his wife have quietly lived
    For fifty years and more.

From the house, which was built before their day,
    They can follow the winding stream
Through meadows as fair as ever beguiled
    A poet in his dream.

They can hear the hum of the waterfall
    And voices from over the lea,
And the distant stroke of the woodman's axe,
    And murmurings of the sea.

'T is seldom within this quiet retreat
    The face of the stranger is seen ;
A stillness, like that of the Sabbath, rests
    Upon its fields of green.

The house, as we enter its time-worn door,
    Has an air of unruffled repose,
Like the hush of a dreamy autumn day
    When nearing to its close.

ONLY WAITING. 107

It speaks of a harvest of gathered sheaves,
   Of reapers with toiling all o'er,
Of hand in hand for a little while yet,
   Till cometh the nevermore.

We feel we are treading on hallowed ground,
   And reverently bow the head,
As we count the years of wedded life
   They have together led.

They only wait for a few more morns,
    For a few more smiles and tears,
When the hands of the clock will cease to move
    In numbering their years.

It is said the house in their early days
    Was known for its music and mirth,
When laughter and song kept time with the roar
    Of fires upon their hearth.

But tears would start should we venture to speak
    Of those who have passed away,
And we deal with these old folks tenderly
    In all we have to say;

For long as the years of their life shall last,
    And memory holdeth its throne,
They will muse on scenes of the buried past
    While living here alone;

And fain would know, as through faith the bliss
    Of the heavenly land appears,
If they'll love each other so fondly there
    As here, for endless years.

We may wander some day along the banks
    Of this river quiet and fair,
And knock at the door, but find no more
    These old folks waiting there.

THE PILGRIM FATHERS.

HOME of my boyhood, wheresoe'er I stray,
A toiler long upon the world's highway,
My heart turns fondly, honored shrine, to
   thee,
In that quaint dwelling near the restless sea, —
Where one bleak winter eve the brave Mayflower,
Sport of the wild waves, subject to their power,
Dropped her small anchor at the set of sun,
Her voyage for truth and conscience-sake well
   done.

Oft, when a boy, upon the hill I've stood,
Where the old homestead leaned against the
   wood,
And looked across the intervening vale
Where prouder barques to-day in triumph sail,
And fancied through what straits the Pilgrims trod
Those desert pathways where they walked with
   God.

Plain, earnest men ! an unbelieving world
Hailed not the banner which they there unfurled;
As they went forth but little could they know
That streams of blessing from their lives would flow;
That from the hut which unpretending raised
Its lowly roof with "HERE LET GOD BE PRAISED,"
A light would break whose radiance afar
Would be to millions as a morning star;
That laws more righteous than the world had known
Would be the product of the seed there sown;
And commonwealths would rise and bless the name,
Of saint and sage then all unknown to fame.

TWILIGHT.

CLOSE not for awhile the shutters;
    Speed not thus departing day:
    It will breathe its choicest blessings
As it glides from time away.

These are hours I prize the highest,
    Moments of the soul's release
From its constant round of duty,
    To that blissful haven, PEACE.

As the gath'ring darkness deepens,
    Twilight, ling'ring in the west,
Bringeth with its benedictions,
    To the heavy-laden, rest.

Ere the vision shall elude us,
    Softer speak the whispered word;
All the fountains of our being
    In this hallowed hour are stirred.

While the fire-lights flame and flicker,
  Memory, busy, now recalls
Gentle forms who round us lingered,
  Like the shadows on the walls.

As upon the dusty highway,
  Now and then, some cool retreat
For a moment lures us thither,
  There to rest our weary feet, —

So the twilight, 'mid the bustle
  Of our busy life imparts
Strength for new and brave endeavor,
  To our weak and fainting hearts.

Wait not, then, but close the shutters;
  Duty beckons to us still;
But the hour has brought us courage
  For our task through good and ill.

BOSTON LIGHT IN NOVEMBER.

 LOOK from my window over the bay;
  The cold east wind has a sorrowful
    tone;
The light of this dreary November day
  Departs, and I 'm left with my thoughts alone.

No star will be seen in the murky skies;
  The sullen clouds hang heavy and low;
Beyond where the shadowy fortress lies,
  The belated sea-gulls wearily go.

The heart has no words in which to express
  Its secret emotions of grief and pain;
The hidden depths of its loneliness, —
  Its longings for something it cannot attain.

But lo! through the gathering mist and gloom,
  The light of a far-away lighthouse gleams;
It enters, a welcome guest, my room,
  With courage emblazoned upon its beams.

And to other hearts afar down the bay,
  Out on the troubled and stormy sea,
To the homeward bound, it has brave words to
    say,
  Even more gladsome than unto me.

Ho, beacon-light on this rock-bound strand !
  I hail thee ever as lover and friend ;
Thou dost take the desolate one by the hand,
  And benisons over the billows send.

No matter how lonely and dark the night,
  Or wildly the tempest-tossed barque may stray,
The ruddy gleams of thy sentinel light,
  Like angels of mercy, glide over the bay.

UPON THE SEA.

TO-NIGHT, O God, upon the sea,
   The sufferer turns his eyes to Thee;
   Through the dark day the howling blast
Has swept with fearful fury past;
And many hearts in wild despair
Have bowed in agony of prayer;
For, tempest tossed, on half a wreck,
The sailor treads the quivering deck :
He prayed that one faint ray of light
Might break the clouds ere came the night;
But now the night is overspread
Upon his poor defenceless head,
And whither can the sailor flee,
Oh, whither, Father, but to Thee !

Just now I dreamed that by my side
He stood in all his manly pride;
I looked upon his earnest face,
Still radiant in its boyhood's grace;

I pressed him to my heart, but lo !
Against the casement beats the snow ;
And through my struggling tears I see
Him clinging to a wreck at sea.

Speak Thou ! and whisper, " Peace be still,"
O Thou ! the waves obey Thy will;
And succor to the needy send,
O Thou ! who art the sufferer's friend ;
And spare to-night upon the sea
The soul that turns, O Lord, to thee !

THE LAST ROBIN.

ET a little longer,
    Robin red-breast, stay;
All thy gay companions
    Long since flew away:
While the groves were vocal
    With their merry chime,
Quickly on the dial
    Moved the hands of Time.

O'er the hazy landscape
    Stand the stacks of grain;
Autumn's golden sentinels
    Marshalled on the plain;
And the shouts of reapers,
    Gathering their sheaves,
Mingle with the rustling
    Of the falling leaves.

Memories tinged with sadness
    Weigh upon the heart,
As with cherished objects
    Tenderly we part;

For the cricket, singing
   At the open door,
Tells us we may never
   Look upon them more.

Then a little longer
   Lingering by the way,
Herald of the spring-time,
   Robin red-breast, stay;
While the shadows lengthen,
   And the earth, grown sere,
Wraps her frosty mantle
   Round the closing year.

SONG OF THE HARVEST.

THE glad harvest greets us, brave toiler
    for bread,
  Good cheer! the prospect is brighter
    ahead;
Like magic, the plentiful sunshine and rain
Have ripened our millions of acres of grain;
And the poorest the wolf may keep from his
    door, —
There'll be bread and to spare another year more.
    So sing merrily, merrily,
      As we gather it in;
    We will store it away gladly,
      In garner and bin.

We hailed with delight, yet tempered with fear,
The corn as it grew from the blade to the ear;
Lest haply, though large is the surplus in store,
That bread might be dearer for twelve months or
    more;

But the sunshine and rain, how they ripened the
  grain
That waited the sickle over hillside and plain !
    So sing merrily, merrily,
      As we gather it in ;
    We will store it away gladly,
      In garner and bin.

Oh, ne'er let us question the Wisdom which guides
Our feet in green pastures, and for us provides ;
Who now, as aforetime, His glory displays,
In the bounty that crowns our autumnal days :
Let the glad tidings echo the continent o'er,
There'll be bread and to spare another year more !
    So sing merrily, merrily,
      As we gather it in ;
    We will store it away gladly,
      In garner and bin.

THE WEEK BEFORE CHRISTMAS.

ROM break of dawn till set of sun,
My house is kept brimful of fun :
Mysterious whisperings are heard ;
In drawers and closets things are stirred ;
I 'm stoutly charged to keep away
From this and that by night and day ;
And if, perchance, I happen in,
My ears are greeted with the din
Of feet, a hurrying to and fro,
Concealing things they dare not show.
And when amid the whirl and clatter
I ask, " Do tell me what 's the matter? "
The answer I am sure to get
Is, " Pray don't be in such a fret !
For only once a year, you know,
Hides Cupid in the mistletoe ;
And by and by, yes, by and by,
You 'll know the merry reason why."

Ah, blithesome torments ! who would miss
These moments of unclouded bliss ?

Or lose this rapture of a child
To be by fairy-sprites beguiled?
Or care to know thy secrets, till
The shout is heard o'er vale and hill,
ON EARTH BE PEACE, GOOD WILL TO MEN,
THE STAR, THE STAR OF BETHLEHEM!

DECEMBER.

WHAT though northern blasts are sweeping
    Over now the frost-bound lea?
    The returning sun is bringing
Hope and cheer for you and me.

We have oft repined while passing
    Through these drear December days;
Now the curtain, slowly rising,
    Turns complaining into praise.

Drifting on — how small our knowledge
    Of the Hand which guards and guides
Our frail barques amid the currents,
    Of life's ever shifting tides!

Sooner than our fancy pictures,
    Robin red-breast, some fine day,
Will be blithely saying to us,
    "Snow and ice have passed away."

So it is, in shine and shadow
    We are hearing words of cheer ;
Never more than when the darkness
    Deepens round the closing year.

How will clouds that still may vex us
    Speed their flight if we remember,
Though some days are dark and dreary,
    'T will not always be December.

THE WAYSIDE REST.

This wayside rest, beneath the spreading tree,
Was meant, O weary traveller, for thee ;
Here take thine ease, and bless the kindly hand
That for thy comfort this good seat hath planned.

ANOTHER YEAR.

NOTHER year? and shall we then
Be found among the marts of men?
Upon life's page will there be still
Some little space for us to fill?
Or will the day of life be o'er,
And we be known as here no more?

Not now may we discern the goal;
So up and on, O earnest soul!
There yet is work for you and me;
The cross before the crown must be;
The Master whom we serve knows best
When, worn and weary, we may rest.

And, brother, as along the race
Of life you reach a higher place,
Enough for me, beneath the hill,
To tread the quiet valley still!
Enough if I may sing a lay,
To charm a passing hour away.

Then let us, with a manly heart,
Each in his way perform his part;
And lift some load, as on we go,
From shoulders bending weak and low;
And leave behind us more than fame —
The record of an honored name.

THE PORTRAIT PAINTER.

He had the skill the lineaments to trace,
And on the canvas paint the human face;
To one bright goal his eyes were ever turned,
To win that prize the fires within him burned;
His work the critics censured more than praised,
Though oft they had his expectations raised;
In unremitting toil he did his best,
Then penniless passed on to his eternal rest.

TO SAMUEL FRANCIS SMITH.

AUTHOR OF "AMERICA."

1808-1888.

DEAR friend of well-remembered years,
    When youth was on thy brow, and mine,
Thy smoothly flowing numbers seemed
    A well-spring from a source Divine.

With undiminished affluence still,
    From the same fountain calm and clear,
Flow melodies as musical
    As dropped upon my boyhood's ear.

Ay, holier are their undertones,
    And richer with the lore of age;
The op'ning vista down the vale
    Grows broader to the saint and sage.

As friends beloved reach one by one
    Life's limit, threescore years and ten,
Thy fingers touch the old-time chords,
    Responsive with their sweet Amens.

For never fairer is the vine
　　Than when its purpling grapes hang low ;
And life's divinest hour is when
　　'T is radiant in its sunset glow.

And thou dost stay the fleeting hours,
　　To paint the blush ere it depart ;
And weave thy benedictions round
　　The holiest tendrils of the heart.

Oh, heavenly gift of poesy !
　　And beautiful, when it doth bless
As thine hath done thy fellow-man,
　　In its embracing tenderness.

As oft a harp will murmur on
　　When the sweet song we sang is o'er,
And charm us with its memories when
　　The hand that swept it is no more, —

So will remembrance of thy life,
　　Its fourscore years of song and cheer,
Like music linger when we miss
　　Thy presence from our pathways here.

ODE.

Celebration of the City of Boston, July 4, 1870.

WHILE hill and valley, stream and shore,
Break forth in songs of joy once more,
We come, the children of the Free,
And bring our tribute, Lord, to thee.

How fair the heritage we claim,
Jehovah, ransomed in Thy name;
Fresh verdure springs along the way
In which Thy people walk to-day.

A sweeter fragrance lingers round
The shrines we hail as holy ground;
And dearer grow the paths we tread,
Above the consecrated dead.

O land of promise! native land!
Serene before the nations stand;
By God inspired to bless the throng
Which press the world's highways along.

From foes reclaimed, by Truth made free.
Thy form shall ever fairer be,
As under His benign control,
The gathering ages onward roll.

LET EVERY HEART REJOICE AND SING.

Sung by children of the Sabbath Schools of Boston in Faneuil Hall, July 4, 1842.

ET every heart rejoice and sing,
   Let the swelling chorus rise ;
   Ye reverend men and children, bring
      To God your sacrifice :
Whilst the breath of the morning floateth
      Along our valleys fair,
And the song of gladness riseth,
      Upon the dewy air, —
   While the rocks and the rills,
   While the vales and the hills,
A glorious anthem raise, —
   Let each prolong
   The grateful song,
And the God of our fathers praise !

Where first the voice of freedom
   Was heard in days of yore,
Now let the children's children
   Repeat that song once more ;

While our Country's banner o'er us
Still waveth proudly free,
Oh, let the exulting chorus
Ascend, great God, to thee:
While the rocks and the rills,
While the vales and the hills,
A glorious anthem raise;
Let each prolong
The grateful song,
And the God of our fathers praise.

TREMONT TEMPLE.

RESTORED once more from out the flames,
As Time rolls on, through good and ill,
Fair Temple! to all noble aims,
We come to consecrate thee still:

To Speech, unfettered as the wind,
To Liberty, restrained by law,
To Charity, for all mankind,
To Visions, such as prophets saw.

For all who seek the lost to find,
And draw them from the paths of sin,
Lift high thy Temple gates, and let
The heralds of Salvation in.

When Science, Learning, Art, and Song
Combine, the throngs to lure and bless,
As glide the favored hours along,
They will not love thine altars less.

O grandly reconstructed walls!
May our glad work and mission be, —
To make more fair, as duty calls,
This much loved city by the sea.

Great Author of the rolling years!
Unchanged, through Time and Space the same,
In every shrine which Goodness rears,
Forever honored is thy name.

October, 1880.

DOMESTIC.

There is no spot in all this wide-spread earth,
He hails more gladly than the quiet hearth,
Who sought for honor, struggled hard for fame,
And grasps the shadow of a fleeting name.

HOME.

Domestic happiness, thou only bliss
Of Paradise that has survived the fall!
Thou art the nurse of Virtue. In thine arms
She smiles, appearing, as in truth she is,
Heaven-born and destined to the skies again!

       Cowper.

O speaks the world — where hearts in union beat,
On the thronged highway or the lonely street,
In the proud palace or the poor man's cot,
Love makes the home, and sanctifies the spot.

The thoughtless youth its quiet charms may spurn,
To other scenes his wayward fancy turn,
And man for pleasure, honor, power, may stray
Far from the landmarks of his boyhood's day —

Yet will his heart, responsive to the past,
Weary with life, oft backward glances cast
Adown the vistas of remembered years,
Illumed by smiles, but oftener dimmed with tears,
And anchor fondly where it spread its sail
To the delusions of the passing gale.

EDEN.

From a poem delivered before the Literary Fraternity of Waterville College, now Colby University, August, 1841.

FAIR was the earth! in vernal beauty drest,
The bright creation of His high behest
Whose power unseen from chaos order made,
The frowning mountain, and the smiling glade,
When man, last formed, yet first beneath the skies,
Devoutly hailed the bliss of Paradise.

The flowers blushed sweetly as each rival hue
Revealed its beauties first to Adam's view;
And softly strayed the cool, delicious air
Among the branches of the cedars there.
The lake that mirrored on its breast that night
The stars of heaven with new-created light,
More glorious still reflected morning's ray,
Which child-like dallied with its virgin spray;
And music woke, far over hill and plain, —
Sounds so melodious may not breathe again.

How blessed amid those Eden bowers to walk,
And free with Nature and her Maker talk !
Still undefiled by spot or stain of sin,
To mar the image of the God within.
Yet not complete ; though Eden bloomed around,
One yearning void in man's lone breast was found ;
And power Divine spake woman into life,
And Adam clasped in Eve his young, enchanting wife.

Now hill and vale in wilder beauty grew,
As hand in hand they hailed the enrapturing view ;
And sweeter flowers still fairer festoons made,
More grateful was the palm-trees' cooling shade,
The murmuring zephyrs breathed a gladder tone,
For Heaven decreed, " Man should not live alone."

Thus came the gift ! and where, O muse, wilt thou
For garlands wander to bedeck thy brow?
Where, in thy flight from whence the vision broke,
When woman smiled and man to bliss awoke,
Where wilt thou pause to gather gems that glow,
The pledge that love yet lingers here below?

As the mild graces of this favored hour,
Steal o'er the senses with bewitching power,
Charmed with the scene, the adventurous muse
    awakes,
And the long silence of her slumber breaks,
While Home, — Sweet Home! the burden of
    her lay,
Breathes from her harp as glide the hours away.

BOY AND MAIDEN.

FROM the ever deep'ning distance
    Of the past, I oft recall
    One whose smile upon my pathway
As a sunbeam seemed to fall;
Who, when dropped the apple blossoms,
    Loved adown the lanes to stray,
Plucking here and there a wild flower,
    Fragrant with the breath of May.

Day by day some fancy lured us
    Where the village pathways met,
I a boy with boundless longings,
    She an artless school-girl yet, —
And this fair and winsome maiden,
    Tripping lightly o'er the lea,
Hidden in her basket often,
    Had a chosen flower for me.

Not a word was ever spoken,
    Very strange to me it seems, —
Not a whisper passed between us,
    Of the burden of our dreams;

Not as lovers' were our meetings,
　　Nor as lovers' our good-byes ;
Only boy and maiden were we,
　　Handsome in each other's eyes.

Many years have come and vanished,
　　And our locks are thin and gray ;
Still she plucks for me the wild flowers,
　　Fragrant with the breath of May :
More than maiden I behold her,
　　With the sunset on her brow,
For as one of God's good angels,
　　She is walking with me now.

'T is sunshiny weather,
Because we're together

THE COTTAGE BONNET.

A SIMPLE cottage bonnet
    she wore,
Of braided straw, in the
    days of yore;
It had a Quakerish look,
    't is true,
With its plain trimmings
    of white and blue ·
But whene'er she thrust her veil aside,
And stood in the bloom of maiden pride,
You could not ask for a face more fair
Than beamed from beneath that bonnet there.

It took the eye of one who now
Looks fondly on that same fair brow;
And often as returns that day,
The last sweet Sabbath morn in May,
He hears again the robin sing,
And sees the lark upon the wing;
The apple-trees are white with bloom,
The air is fragrant with perfume.

A simple cottage bonnet still
Doth all his waning pulses thrill,
And wakens the remembered lays
That sanctified those early days.

And when upon the crowded streets
The matron and the maid he meets
With shapeless hats and tangled curls,
He oft recalls the modest girls
Who tripped along at even-tide,
Unvexed by fashion's pomp and pride;
And her who was his virgin bride,
Who, walking with him down the hill,
Could wear a cottage bonnet still,
And be as fair and sweet to-day
As on that rosy morn in May.

EARLY AND LATER LOVE.

I COULD not know, as swift the years,
  My dear, their ceaseless cycles run,
  And smiles are often changed to tears,
As visions vanish one by one,

That now my heart would cling to thine
  As never in life's early morn;
For though that love seemed all divine,
  'T was not of this deep fulness born.

Our early love was as the blush
  Of the young morning bright and gay;
Our later love is as the hush,
  When sunset shadows glide away.

The peace of life's calm eventide
  Befits the furrowed brow of age:
And love, by memories sanctified,
  Is an abiding heritage.

Adown the vale the nearer view
   Of heaven dispels the lingering fear,
As hand in hand we still pursue
   The onward path of duty here.

Oh, it were well, when conflicts cease,
   And toil and turmoil vex no more,
Beside life's gathered sheaves in peace,
   To live its checkered journey o'er.

Though adverse winds awhile may blow,
   And clouds their shadows o'er us cast,
There 's something tells me that the bow
   Of Hope will span our sky at last.

Oh, early love and later love !
   One, through the years which God hath given,
A glimpse and foretaste from above
   Of the perfected love of heaven.

OUR OLD HOMESTEAD.

AS a landmark quaint and hoary,
   Still to me the old house stands,
   Half concealed by trees around it,
From the fragrant meadow lands.

There my sires for generations
   Hailed the coming of the sun —
There they rested from their labors,
   When their daily task was done.

Few and simple were their longings,
   Frugal was their honest fare,
And that gentle maid, Contentment,
   Was a constant presence there.

From a brook which never failed them
   They drew water day by day,
While its music gladdened ever
   All the banks along its way.

There the lilacs blossomed early,
　　There the corn its tassels waved,
There the barn was filled with plenty,
　　When the storms of winter raved.

All its pathways in my boyhood
　　Led to pastures fair and sweet;
Oh, how oft have they been trodden
　　By my bare and restless feet.

Stranger, you may find this homestead
　　Near the spot the Pilgrims prest,
When the Mayflower bore her burden
　　Where the weary might find rest.

Should you scan its plain surroundings,
　　And inquire the reason why
I have lured you for a moment
　　From your way while passing by —

'T is to show you, O my brother.
　　Wandering the wide world round,
That in such retreats the truest
　　Source of earthly bliss is found.

STARTING IN LIFE.

 OFT recall that well-remembered day,
Which brightly dawned upon my boyhood's way,
When leaving home I crossed the village green,
Just as the sun above the hills was seen.

My simple pack, my treasured all, was there,
Laden with tokens of a mother's care,
With gifts affection's loving hands had brought,
Some dear memento that a sister wrought,
Some modest gem the giver prayed might be
Bound to my heart for "Aye remember me."

"God keep thy spirit pure and undefiled;
God's blessing rest upon thy path, my child,"
Was her adieu who evermore would hold
In her embrace the first son of her fold.
And as I lingered at the open door
For one last kiss, for one fond good-by more,
The little birds their sweetest farewell sang,
The dim old woods with farewell echoes rang,

STARTING IN LIFE.

The sparkling rills sent up a farewell sigh,
The drooping willows softly breathed, " Good-by,"
And brier, and fern, and dewy scented flower
Joined in the farewells of that parting hour.

I wandered slowly through the crowded street,
But caught no smile from all I chanced to meet ;
A homesick boy on life's uncertain way,
To win esteem or go, alas ! astray.
The city's din, its scenes so strange and new,
Passed like a dream before my wondering view,
And silver lays from fairy harps were sung,
And Pleasure wooed me with her flattering tongue.

'T was then I felt that some restraining power
Seemed to be near me in the trying hour ;
When for the Right I wished unmoved to stand,
I felt the pressure of a helping hand ;
When to my lips was brought the cup of bliss,
Upon my cheek I felt my mother's kiss ;
And strength sufficient for the day was given, —
Oh, still they lure my erring feet to heaven.

THANKSGIVING EVE.

MY boyhood's home before me lies,
    Just as it looked when life was young,
    Ere I had spread my tiny sail,
Or to the breeze my pennons flung;
The blue smoke climbs the hill beside,
    The brook goes singing on its way,
And voices near and far proclaim,
    The coming of Thanksgiving Day.

A thousand welcomes, as of old,
    Ring out upon the frosty air,
While through the orchard boughs I see
    The village lights reflected there;
To-morrow will be festal time,
    And city halls and hamlets low
Will echo to the merry chimes,
    And memories of long ago.

We all are young who gather here, —
 The sire of three-score years and ten
Trips lightly with his sweet grandchild,
 The gayest of our youngest men;
For who cares aught for wrinkles now,
 Or sighs because his locks are gray?
His heart beats light who hails with me
 The feasts of our Thanksgiving Day.

Now let me slumber once again
 In that old chamber in the Ell,
And wake up from my dreams, and hear
 The night-winds through the casement swell;
No monarch has a grander couch,
 Or softer down on which to rest,
Than mine will be, for oh, my friends,
 I'm once more in my boyhood's nest!

THE SCHOOL-BOY'S VACATION.

IS trunk was packed for days before;
   The blood coursed quickly through his
     veins;
The hours he counted o'er and o'er,
   As counts the captive in his chains:
     His task was finished — why delay
     The eagle in his upward way?

He rose ere morn illumed the skies;
   The clock had only rung out three;
It was an early hour to rise,
   But not an early hour for thee,
     O boy! for in thy dreams all night,
     How loomed the promised land in sight!

Thou wert away among the hills;
   Where mountains rear their lofty heads;
Where sweetly sing the crystal rills,
   And green banks fringe the river beds;
     Where flocks, and herds, and bird, and bee
     A thousand welcomes gave to thee.

THE SCHOOL-BOY'S VACATION.

O boy! I would that, free as thou,
   I, too, might sweep o'er hill and plain; —
Without a wrinkle on my brow,
   Live over life's young morn again;
      And pack my trunk, and rise at three,
      And start at eight, along with thee.

THE TROUBLE OF THE HOUSE.

THEY name her " Trouble of the House,"
   My merry little one,
And tell large stories of the deeds
   Her busy hands have done ;

That every room has its own tale
   Of mischief to declare,
Of eyes which peer exceeding bright
   Through locks of golden hair.

I don't believe one-half they say ;
   And if I did, what then ?
Why, simply that her little life
   Was bubbling up again ;

That one more ray of sunlight streamed
   Through this fair world of ours ;
That one more bud was blossoming,
   Within our garden bowers.

True, wrecks of many a toy and gem
    Lie scattered on the floor:
And little feet come pattering
    Through every open door;

And tireless as the bee which culls
    Its honey from the flower,
Her mind, with curious wonderings filled,
    Is busy every hour.

But we as soon the streams may turn
    Which to the ocean roll,
As quench this spark that glows and burns
    In an immortal soul.

The wish to know the why and when,
    The mystery to explore,
The will to dare the path to tread
    We have not trod before —

Rules both alike the man and child,
    The simple and the wise;
Both chase the bubble as it flits
    Before their eager eyes;

Both sport with trifles, — bat and ball
    Are in our hands alway;
And longings never satisfied
    Attend us day by day.

Then chide her not, but rather let
　　Her glad heart soar and sing;
The dew is fresh upon her brow,
　　Be freedom on her wing.

We hail the promise of to-day;
　　For, if the ruddy glow
Of morning breaks upon us such,
　　What may the evening show!

TO N. AT THIRTY-TWO.

THOU still art dear, as day by day
I press along life's lengthening way,
As dear as when thy infant smile
Could all my weary hours beguile,
Or when thy foot, in girlhood's glee,
Tripped lightly over hill and lea.

I cannot but esteem thee more
As I review the journey o'er,
And see how that sweet life of thine
Has cheered and blessed the half of mine.

I would the sea did not divide
Thy gentle presence from my side ;
That I might know this morn the bliss,
Of leaving on thy brow a kiss.

And yet these leagues of raging sea
Which roll between thyself and me,

Shall bear the prayer that God will bless
Thy coming years as mine grow less,
And ever make thy life as true
As now, dear child, at thirty-two!

VENTNOR, ISLE OF WIGHT.

MARIA.

CHILD of the fair and open brow,
    My heart clings closely up to thine,
    As in thy eyes enthroned I see,
  The tokens of a love divine.
No voice of bird or summer bee
    Is sweeter than thy guileless speech;
No op'ning blossom of the Spring,
    Doth purer lines of goodness teach.

From morn till eve thy quiet ways,
    Have the same artless tale to tell;
Within thy ever loving breast,
    The sweetest thoughts of goodness dwell:
And when I mark thy winning smile,
    The tears will oft unbidden start,
As clinging closer, still I press
    Thine angel presence to my heart.

Child of my love! this changing world
    Oft throws its shadows o'er my way;
And turning weary from its scenes,
    I long to reach some quiet bay;—

Some haven, where the strife of earth
  Will not oppress my spirit so ;
Where kindred hearts speak words of cheer,
  As on to duty still we go.

That haven is the glad hearthstone,
  At which thy foot in childhood's glee
Doth bound, to greet my coming home,
  As shadows lengthen o'er the lea.
Here ever, as a vesper star,
  A loving light of beauty shed,
As evening shades around me close,
  The angel of the path I tread.

OUR CHILD.

 GIFT from Heaven, — our joy and stay,
She grew in beauty day by day,
And oft we sought with all things fair
Her gentle presence to compare,
And loved her more as Time revealed
The worth her modesty concealed;
So thoughtful, true, and undefiled, —
From maid to matron, still our child.

So like the passing of a dream
Was her sweet life, she 'll ever seem
Unchanged, — a child upon my knee,
With loving arms embracing me;
A morning star, whose lingering ray
Made beautiful the dawn of day,
Then melted into light away.

OUR HOUSEHOLD PET.

EAR pet of our household, sober and gray,
STRAWBERRY FINCH, thou art passing
away;
Thirteen long years from thy Indian nest, —
Beautiful bird ! it is time thou shouldst rest.

Scarce to the perch can thy crippled feet cling,
Fainter the song thou art striving to sing,
The half-opened seed drops out from thy bill,
And yet thou art ling'ring here with us still.

She who so loved thee has passed from our eyes,
Under the hillocks her gentle form lies ;
Nevermore here will she list to thy strain, —
Why should we wish thee with us to remain?

Bear to her, bird of the plumage so fair,
Bear to her love Time cannot impair ;
Tell her we long for her loving embrace,
And the smile which played over her angelic face.

Nay, nay, tiny songster, we'll not let thee go,
There is joy in thy presence, a balm for our woe;
With each quivering note of thy half-uttered lay,
Comes the voice of our darling, O birdie, to-day!

TO A. AT TWENTY-ONE.

YOU ask of me, my child, a lay,
Befitting this your natal day, —
A simple song, warm from the heart,
As you with girlhood's morning part,
And venture forth through storm, and strife,
Upon the untried voyage of life.

I'm sitting here beside the sea,
The winds of May blow over me ;
And many a ship with spreading sail
Greets gladly now the fav'ring gale :
The sailor casts one fond look more,
As fast recedes his native shore,
And breathes a blessing, warm and free,
For those he never more may see.

So, I behold you starting now,
With youth still lingering on your brow,
With sails all set and pennons free,
Just out upon the open sea ;

And fancy that your heart turns o'er
Its leaves of memory, as the shore
Recedes from sight, as day by day,
Your barque speeds on its destined way.

Dear child! may ever some good guide,
Be present with you side by side, —
Some pilot, till, all wand'ring o'er,
Your feet have gained the farther shore;
Some loving hand to lead the way,
Through the bright realms of perfect day.

Eastbourne, English Channel.

A SUNBEAM.

HAVE you ever met her skipping,
   Bounding off in play,
   The jolliest of all creatures,
The gayest of the gay?
No bird has lighter pinions,
   Or heart more glad and free;
She's never still a minute,
   But she's very dear to me.

Her black eyes sparkle brightly,
   Her cheeks are rosy red,
Her hat sits very queerly
   'Mong the curls upon her head;
Her frock bears certain witness
   That somebody will sigh,
When they see the rents and tatters
   And that twinkle in her eye.

Dear, busy little body,
   With sunshine in thy heart,
Full of mischief and of goodness,
   A paradox thou art;

A SUNBEAM.

I could fill a volume counting
   Thy many failings o'er,
And yet it is my weakness
   To love thee more and more.

This world is full of sorrow,
   But none beclouds thy way;
There is weeping with the smiling
   In all our homes to-day;
But what canst thou of sorrow,
   My darling, know or care,
With the sunlight on thy pinions,
   And thy spirit free as air?

THY NAME.

To R. P.

THE world may say thy Scripture name
    Doth not befit thy merry youth;
    But 't is a wreath of filial fame,
Inwoven with thy tresses, Ruth.

It has a fragrance all its own,
    And we will fondly hope, forsooth,
'T will honor thee when older grown,
    As once the Hebrew maiden, Ruth.

For even now thy speaking eyes
    And nut-brown cheeks reveal the truth
That much of hidden beauty lies
    Within thy loving bosom, Ruth.

God shield thee with His tender care
    Through all the perils of thy youth;
And make thy eve of life as fair
    As is its cloudless morning, Ruth.

SONG OF THE CHIP-BIRD.

WHEN the early flowers were blooming
    All around my cottage door,
Came a little chip-bird, singing
    To his gentle mate once more;
And his song was full of meaning
    And of gladness unto me,
"Let us build our nest, my darling,
    In this arbor-vitae tree."

It seemed strange that they had chosen
    Near our door to make their nest;
But they sought not for our guidance
    In this matter of their quest.
So his song for days that followed
    Had a gracious charm for me,
"Let us build our nest, my darling,
    In this arbor-vitae tree."

When June came with smiles and roses,
    Sat the chip-bird on her nest;
And a brood of birdlings nestled
    Closely to her downy breast;

There, with love that knew no changing,
　They were nourished day by day,
Till, their tiny wings unfolding,
　To the fields they flew away.

Now the summer sun is waning,
　Drowsy is the cricket's tune,
Still my heart is with the chip-birds,
　And the rosy month of June :
For they came like rays of sunlight,
　Singing round my cottage door ;
And my heart the blessing pondereth,
　For its good forevermore.

AN EPISTLE FROM THE RHINE.

To M.

E are here, but not with thee,
Thou, who art beyond the sea;
Whose delight it was to trace
Scenes of beauty and of grace,
In the river rushing by;
In the rainbow-tinted sky;
In the soft wind's lullaby;
Thou, who never canst forget,
How the bright sun rose and set,
On that day when like a dream,
We passed swiftly down the stream.
By full many a storied shrine,
Of the castellated Rhine;
When the grand Cathedral towers
Cast their shadows over ours;
Those were halcyon days, my child,
All serene and undefiled.

But a fleeting hour ago,
When the sun was waning low,
In the dreamy town of Bonn,
Quietly we looked upon
Those fair heights, the seven hills,
Which the stranger's bosom thrills,
Sailing up the fairy Rhine,
River worshipped as divine.

Grandly through the purple haze,
Of these sweet autumnal days,
Rise their summits, evermore
Guarding there the mystic shore.
Was it fancy, as farewell
From our lips reluctant fell,
That beneath the evening sky,
They too waved to us, " Good-by!"

COLOGNE, 1878.

OUR COTTAGE HOME. No. 1.

It was a cherished desire of mine during a prolonged absence in Europe in the years 1877-8-9, to have on my return home a rural residence, where my family and friends could come and enjoy, with us, the pleasures of domestic life.

HOPE, whenever I return,
Dear native land to thee !
To have a cot where I may dwell,
By riverside or lea ;
Whose charm should be its home-like look,
And unpretending air,
Yet something which might grow to be
A thing of beauty there.

With other comforts, it should have
    An open fire of wood;
A daily paper, some choice books,
    And simple country food:
I 'd have a dog, perhaps a poll,
    And just enough of ground
For flowers to blossom at their will,
    With ivy climbing round,
In this retreat I would not care
    For what the world might say,
If my small cot should only lure,
    Some loving hearts that way.

Our poet sages long ago
    These simple truths proclaimed:
Man's life is but a fleeting show,
    Howe'er it may be named;
And more of health and happiness
    Is found in hut than hall;
And our dear Father sendeth down
    His rain alike on all.

The cottage that my fancy paints,
    Though small indeed it be,
Will be enough, if large enough
    For M. C. L. and me:

There let it blow, or high or low,
  Let sunshine come or rain,
We'll comfort take whilst humming oft
  Some old familiar strain.
With thankful hearts, unvexed by care,
  We'll pass life's evening days,
Unnoticed by the throngs which press
  Along the world's highways.

Should the dear children of our love,
  Come here with us to dine,
There'll be a slice, I'm sure, for each,
  But more of *l'eau* than wine ;
And our small cot will stretch enough
  To hold the whole of mine.

DRESDEN, 1878.

OUR COTTAGE HOME. No. 2.

HEN the trailing sweet arbutus,
 Peeps from underneath the snow,
 And the rills by frosts unfettered,
Onward to the rivers flow, —

Then, O builder of our cottage,
 Set its corner-stone with care,
And begin that thing of beauty,
 Which my fancy pictures there.

Let the summer sun, advancing,
 See the progress that it makes ;
Rounding into full completeness
 When the peach its crimson takes.

Now begin thy gentle mission,
 Daughter with the speaking eyes ;
Deck its halls and chambers deftly,
 From thy storehouse of supplies ;

Bring your garlands and mementos,
  Gathered on a foreign shore ;
They'll remind us of the by-ways
  That our feet have travelled o'er :

Ivy, from old castle ruins,
  Alpine flowers from Switzerland,
Views of crystal lakes and mountains,
  Pebbles from the ocean strand ;

Place them all about the dwelling,
  In and out of cosey nooks ;
They will teach us better lessons
  Than we ever learn from books.

Busy thus, thy comely sister,
  Sharer of thy griefs and joys,
Will the cottage set in order
  For the coming of the boys.

Gather now, O loved and loving,
  Children of life's early morn !
Ye who to a golden future
  In our dreams of life were born —

Gather once more at our fireside,
    Let the old-time laugh ring out,
Whilst relating to each other
    What your hands have been about:

Bring with you your buds and blossoms,
    Bring the firstlings of your flock,
Bring the keys which softly, gently,
    All the treasured past unlock, —

And whilst heart with heart communeth,
    Should a struggling tear-drop fall,
It will be that we remember
    How the Lord hath blessed us all.

Thus my fancy paints our cottage;
    Thus to me it seems to stand
'Mid the green lanes of my boyhood,
    In our own, my native land;

Sanctifying all the landscape,
    Cosey as a song-bird's nest, —
When, O builder will you build it?
    For my spirit longs for rest.

LONDON, February, 1879.

META.

ETA, gentle Meta,
    When the day was done,
    Sat upon the doorsteps,
Singing, one by one,
Simple cradle lullabies,
    Tinkling like the rill,
While the sun was sinking
    Underneath the hill.

Happy little Meta
    Knew not that so soon,
Over the cedar groves,
    Up would rise the moon;
That the stars would twinkle
    Merrily and bright,
While her lips were murmuring,
    Lovingly, " Good-night."

So our merry Meta,
    When the sun had set,
And the clover meadows
    With the dews were wet,

On her couch lay sleeping
    As the lilies sleep,
When, above the valleys,
    Stars their vigils keep.

Ah, dear little Meta!
    Who that evening knew,
As the Night her mantle
    Round the wide world drew.
That a deeper shadow
    On our hearts would lie.
When the stars of morning
    Faded from the sky?

Who, of all that loved thee,
    Knew one vacant chair
Now would wait thy presence
    At the hour of prayer;
That our feet would linger
    Round the open door,
Waiting for thy coming,
    Coming, nevermore?

Meta, angel Meta!
    Waiting still we stand,
Weary,—oh, how weary!
    On the ocean strand,

Catching, 'mid the pauses
  Of the billow's roar,
Echoes from the voices
  On the farther shore;
Waiting, longing, yearning,
  For thy smile once more,
Waiting, for that greeting, darling,
  On the farther shore!

MARY.

*I knelt to take a brother's farewell kiss,
And knew that we had parted.*

 LINK is broken in the chain,
   A soul hath passed away,
   A lute that breathed so sweet a strain
For us hath hushed its lay :
A seat is vacant at our board,
   A place beside our hearth,
And grief, that ne'er before was stirred,
   Has dimmed the joys of earth.

O Mary : can my shattered lyre
   A requiem sing for thee?
Can I whose cherished hopes expire
   Attune its chords for thee?
Thy presence I can still recall,
   Thy smile — I see it now,
And softly doth the sunlight fall
   Upon thy gentle brow ;

Thy step is lightest in the ring,
   Thy laugh is wild and free,
But more, I may not, cannot sing, —
   How can I sing of thee?
O thou, so early absent here,
   So quickly passed to heaven,
What better than the silent tear
   Can to thy praise be given?

Around the spot where thou art laid
   The wild flowers bud and bloom;
The robin sings his morning lay
   Beside thy lowly tomb;
And whispering winds, and winds that sweep
   From off the raging sea,
Blow softer when we come to weep,
   Who oft have wept with thee.

Here, Mary, rest, as come and go
   The seasons in their flight,
As far removed from mortal woe
   As darkness from the light;
As far removed — but not so far
   But faith, with trusting eyes,
Beholds thee, O thou rising star,
   Ascending in the skies!

SHINE AND SHADOW.

THE sky by clouds is overcast,
    And sadness rests on vale and hill;
  Yet comes there in the ling'ring blast
Of Autumn pleasant music still.

Not this a time to roam where smiles
    The landscape clad in vernal bloom;
A lovelier scene the hour beguiles,
    And sheds its sunlight through the gloom.

Away with sorrow! let no thought
    Of coming care becloud the brow;
Affection hath her chaplet wrought,
    And breathes her holiest blessings now.

Who heeds the fury of the blast,
    Or deems November sad and drear,
That shares the bliss of a repast
    Such as love spreads before us here?

Roll on, old year! there's good and ill
    In every cup we drink below;
Some smile will bless our pathway still,
    As shine and shadow come and go.

DEVOTIONAL.

KEEP thy heart right and thou wilt be
Ready ever on land or sea,
To follow the Christ of Galilee.

O who would such a blessing miss?
Or fail to know the untold bliss
Which cometh with His hallowed kiss!

CHRIST-LIKE.

HE doth well whose life is daily
 Sanctified by some good deed,
 Of unselfish love or valor, —
Something, in the hour of need.

Want and woe are near us ever, —
 Whereso'er our feet may tread,
There a burden may be lifted
 From some weak and fainting head,
For His sake, if we are willing
 By the Master to be led.

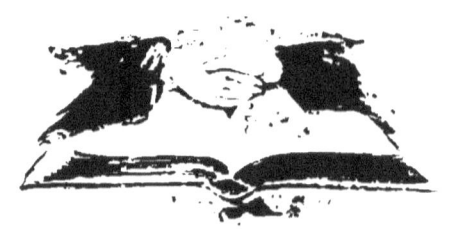

ONE.

That they all may be one. — JOHN xvii. 21.

N that hour by all forsaken,
  Mingling with "Thy will be done,"
Was the Saviour's supplication
  That His people might be one —

One, in all the Christian graces
  Which make life divinely sweet;
One, when as His well-belovéd,
  They should for His service meet.

If that love so all-embracing,
  As he passed through Kedron's vale,
Moved to-day the hosts of Zion,
  How would peace o'er strife prevail!

Metes and bounds are parting ever
    Hearts that would in union blend;
In the name of Truth entailing
    Pain and conflict without end.

With contention in her borders,
    Over formulas and creeds,
Zion oft is shorn of beauty,
    When for righteousness she pleads!

Still, amid conflicting dogmas,
    More and more I seem to hear
God in Christ revealed, — a message
    Welcome to the list'ning ear:

Saying to discordant factions,
    All of questionings aside,
" Here upon this Rock of Ages,
    In fraternal peace abide."

For this unity of spirit
    May I evermore be strong;
Whilst the all-abounding goodness
    Of Jehovah is my song.

Let me haste to lift the burden
    From my neighbor faint and sore,
Feed the hungry, clothe the naked,
    From my more abundant store, —

And the way my feet should travel
    Must be ever plain to me;
I can never err, dear Master,
    When I follow none but Thee.

THE GLAD ASSURANCE.

IF in hours of pain and conflict
   Come these gracious words to me,
   Full of tenderness and pity, —
As thy day thy strength shall be.

Not a sparrow ever falleth,
   Nor a lamb bewildered stray,
But His loving arms infold them,
   As they shelter me to-day.

Ere the bruisèd reed is broken
   He will deign to hear my prayer,
That no trial shall befall me
   Greater than the heart can bear.

In what way relief I plead for
   Is to come, I may not see ;
'T is enough, Divine Compassion
   Will the burden lift from me.

Oh, the peace this promise bringeth !
   All of doubt and fear aside,
That my trusting heart may ever
   In His boundless love confide.

THE GRAVE OF THE DAIRYMAN'S DAUGHTER.

DEAR maiden, in my western home,
  Beyond the ever restless sea,
  In life's young morn I read the tale
The village rector told of thee.

That story of thy lowly life
  So greatly charmed the Christian world
That it became, in every land,
  A banner of the cross unfurled.

And musing on these hallowed scenes,
  Which still the stranger's feet beguile,
I oft have longed to tread, as now,
  The green lanes of this sea-girt isle.

So tenderly were they portrayed,
  In lines the pastor's pencil drew,
Its way-side flowers for thy dear sake,
  Methought, in wilder beauty grew.

A sanctifying Presence reigned
   In all its groves — on hill and lea;
I even seemed to walk with Him
   Who trod the shores of Galilee.

Oh, simple tale of trusting love!
   Meek record of redeeming grace!
What beauty lingers round that spot
   Where Christ hath made a dwelling-place!

And so I come, — not with the blush
   Of morning still upon my brow,
But weary with life's length'ning march,
   I kneel beside thy green grave now.

Yet, with an inner, clearer light,
   To me at this calm moment given,
I see again the narrow way
   By which thy spirit passed to heaven.

And pausing here beyond the din
   And turmoil of the world's highways,
I catch the spirit of these scenes,
   Which filled the preacher's heart with praise:

That faithful teacher, who thy hand,
   Held in his own, as down the vale
Thy gentle spirit leaned upon
   Those promises which never fail, —

With him I tread these breezy downs;
   I trace the lines of shore and sea;
The quiet beauty of these vales,
   All, all, is now revealed to me!

Henceforth, as shadows thicker fall,
   And evening gathers round my way,
With firmer faith my soul will cling
   To Him who was thy staff and stay.

In that dear sacrifice I hail
   Enough for all, enough for me!
Rock of eternal ages Thou!
   O Lamb of God, on Calvary!

Isle of Wight, August, 1877.

SHE HATH DONE WHAT SHE COULD.

[Mark xiv. 8.]

STILL beautiful along the line
   Of deeds well done, this record lives;
   And with an energy divine,
New strength to modest labor gives.

She did not know her Lord would place
   So fair a crown upon her brow;
That in this sentence we should trace
   So much of simple beauty now.

'T was love that moved her hands to pour
   On His dear head the perfumed oil;
And love for Him hath o'er and o'er
   Inspired his servants for new toil.

"Done what she could," — O trusting heart,
   No monumental shaft or shrine
Bears witness to a nobler part,
   A fairer heritage, than thine!

Be such my unobtrusive aim —
Life's golden moments to redeem ;
The smile of God is more than fame,
However fair that prize may seem.

THE STILL SMALL VOICE.

There is a voice to which the heart must listen,
    Where'er in life our erring feet may go ;
A still small voice, whose whisperings we may never
    Tell to another, and alone can know.

And so there comes the doubting and the chiding
    Of souls who fain would aid us on our way :
They cannot hear that hidden, silent mandate,
    We oft may question, but still must obey.

STORM ON THE SABBATH.

NOT many to thy sacred feasts,
   O Zion of our God ! to-day
   Will upward haste with willing feet
Their early sacrifice to pay.
A few — the strong in manhood's might,
   And woman — venturesome for prayer,
And youth — as buoyant as the light,
May mingle in devotion there.

O Sabbath, to my soul most blest !
   Though clothed in sadness and in storm ;
Thou bringest to the weary, rest,
   As if thou cam'st in milder form —
I hailed thee when thy mellow light
   Bathed spire and tree, and vale and hill,
When every scene that charmed the sight,
   In quiet whispered, " Peace, be still."

And now as howls the angry blast,
    And thickly falls the drenching rain,
Faith sees the bow of promise cast
    Athwart the brow of heaven again;
And something in this hour of strife,
    Through all the paths our feet have trod,
Proclaims, amid destruction, life!
    Amid the frowns, the smile of God!

EASTER.

OVER all the hills of God,
   Long by sage and prophet trod,
   One triumphant pæan swells
In the peals of Easter bells.

Breathe, O breath of Love Divine !
On this waiting soul of mine ;
Let all fear be rolled away
From my burdened heart to-day.

Paschal Lamb for sinners slain,
Here without a rival reign ;
Dearer than all else beside,
With me evermore abide.

As life's devious paths I tread,
By Thy constant Presence led,
I shall more than conqueror be,
O my risen Lord ! through Thee.

IN THE SANCTUARY.

"The peace of God which passeth all understanding."

AM longing for the blessing of the peace of God to-day,
O master at the organ, as thy fingers softly stray
O'er its keys, for they are whispering, "Here's a refuge from the strife,
From the trouble and the turmoil of this constant round of life;
Take the blessing freely offered as before His throne you kneel,
Who would now His gracious presence to thy waiting soul reveal."

I've come a suppliant weary from a world of toil and care,
Seeking respite from its bondage in this hallowed hour of prayer,

For release from sordid passions, for grace the
    goal to win,
As my feet are pressing forward through this
    wilderness of sin;
And whilst silently the tear-drops from their
    hidden fountains start,
Touch the chords that surest vibrate with the
    yearnings of my heart.

No care have I to listen to the pæans of the
    choir,
Airs that breathe of sins forgiven better answer
    my desire;
I have naught to plead of merit, my unworthi-
    ness I see, —
Let the peace my spirit craveth, O my Father,
    rest on me.

WINTER EVENING HYMN.

OVER my hearth and home to-night,
   Peace spreads her fair and gentle wing,
And hearts as buoyant as the light
   Their gifts of love and kindness bring.

No pinching want my eyes behold,
   No haggard look, no sunken eye,
No mourner here, whose griefs untold
   Deep in the stricken bosom lie.

I hear the blasts of Winter sweep
   Along the icy-sheeted plain,
Whose wail is sad to them who keep
   Lone watch where Want and Sorrow reign.

But unto me 't is music all,
   The lamp of love burns brightly here,
And softly now as snowflakes, fall
   Kind words upon the list'ning ear.

And yet, O God! this very day,
   My heart has sighed for something more,
Nor knew, beneath such gentle sway,
   Its cup of bliss was running o'er.

THE VILLAGE CHURCH.

T stands where it stood in the olden time,
When my step was light in my boy-
hood's prime,
And I hear, on the breath of the morning swell,
Again the peal of that old church bell.

It stands where it stood on the brow of the hill,
And strangers to me tread its dim aisles still,
While I look around and inquire where
Are the good old folks who once worshipped there?

And they point to the graveyard close by the way,
And tell me they've been there for many a day;
That the manly heart and the blushing maid
Were long ago in that churchyard laid.

There was one I remember, whose mild blue eye
Met tenderly mine as he breathed, "Good-by,"
And the clasp of his hand was warm and true, —
But he wasted away like the morning dew.

Oh, my heart is sad, old church, as I gaze
Around for the friends of my early days,
And my tears fall fast as the April rain,
For I seek the departed here in vain.

CLOSE OF THE WEEK.

PAUSE, my soul! a week hath ended, —
 One the less for thee below;
In this week there have been blended,
 Hope and fear, and joy and woe;
Weary heart, thou canst not murmur,
 O'er thy sky a bow is cast;
One week to thy haven nearer,
 Courage gather from the past.

Pause, my soul! a week hath ended,
 What its record borne for thee?
Whom oppressed hast thou befriended?
 Who the happier been for thee?
Hast thou love for hate requited?
 To thy neighbor wert thou true?
What, my soul, hast thou neglected
 What performed thou shouldst not do?

Pause, my soul! a week hath ended,
　Time is bearing thee away;
Only for awhile extended,
　Is the life we live to-day.
What may be upon the morrow,
　God in mercy hides from thee;
But so live, come joy or sorrow,
　As thy day thy strength shall be.

"JESUS CHRIST HIMSELF."

[Ephesians ii. 20.]

WHAT, pastor and guide, is thy message
    to-day?
Through the mazes of sin I have wan-
    dered astray;
Now, weary and worn, I am seeking to find
In this Sabbath repose some rest for the mind.

No speech, howe'er finished its logic or lore,
Can meet my heart's longings — I'm yearning
    for more;
For something unsullied by contact with sin,
The joy of forgiveness, the witness within.

There is an old story, yet evermore new;
On my prodigal heart it distils as the dew;
It tells of redemption for sinners undone,
Through the sacrifice made by the crucified One.

You cannot exhaust it, no plummet nor line
Hath sounded the depths of this ocean divine ;
It rolls round the world, it laves every shore,
And will, through the ages, till time is no more.

Then lead us, O teacher, where the infant Christ
    lay ;
In the paths that He trod let us travel to-day ;
And my heart will rejoice as enthronéd I see
My Saviour, Redeemer, still pleading for me !

"TRUST IN ME."

OH, think not thou art all unblest,
    Though waves of sorrow o'er thee roll;
The saddest heart by grief opprest
    Is under the Divine control.

He who doth mark the sparrow's fall,
    In tender mercy bends to thee:
He throws His shield around us all,
    And sweetly whispers, "Trust in me."

Thou hast no pain unknown to Him,
    Nor canst thou from His presence stray;
And ere the cup o'erflows its brim,
    He'll gently wipe thy tears away.

Then in His hands submissive lie,
    Whose smile can soothe the keenest sorrow;
The rainbow spans the darkest sky,
    And Hope points brightly to the morrow.

THE PASTOR'S RECEPTION.

E gladly gather here to-night,
    Pastor and guide, as children come,
    When the long summer day is o'er,
To the endearing rest of home.

Our restless feet have wandered far,
    And, weary with life's dizzy play,
We hear thy voice as sunset throws
    Its length'ning shadows o'er our way.

A pilgrim band with sandals worn,
    And dust upon our crest and shield,
Thy hallowed message lures us where
    The pastures heavenly verdure yield.

And so we come, and sire and child
    Their offerings and their garlands bring,
And wreathe the winter frost-work with
    The opening blossoms of the spring.

And youth and age, inspired by love,
　Shall tread the path of duty still ;
And fill life's yet unwritten page
　With deeds of mercy and good-will.

And thou anew wilt gather strength,
　Through Him who hath the wine-press trod,
To lead us erring children up
　To the dear City of our God.

So shall the hour be blest, and we,
　Girding our loins for sterner strife,
Will wrestle for that prize which crowns
　His head who wins eternal life !

OUR SANCTUARIES.

"Our feet shall stand within thy gates, O Jerusalem." —
Ps. cxxii. 2.

OH, brothers, toiling weak and worn,
   By sin beset, how oft our eyes
   Turn from these earthly temples, to
The fairer temple in the skies.

We call ours beautiful; but when
   Compared with that by angels trod,
How all unworthy seem the shrines
   We fain would consecrate to God.

Yet He doth deign to meet us here,
   And so refresh us by His grace,
That His abounding love in all
   The changing scenes of life we trace.

What hath been, evermore shall be;
   A golden heritage awaits
The man who walks before the Lord,
   Jerusalem, within thy gates.

ROCK OF AGES.

IN the service of the Sabbath,
   Borne upon seraphic wings,
To my over-burdened spirit
  Comes the song the church choir sings:
    "Rock of Ages, cleft for me,
    Let me hide myself in Thee."

Yes, my heart responsive answers,
   As I join the hallowed strain,
And behold the Man of Sorrows,
   On the cross for sinners slain, —
    "Let the water and the blood,
    From Thy riven side that flowed,
    Be of sin the double cure,
    Cleanse me from its guilt and power."

Yes, my heart again respondeth,
   Let the work be wholly Thine;
I can plead Thy merits only,
   Thou Incarnate Love Divine;

"Could my tears forever flow,
Could my zeal no languor know,
All for sin could not atone,
Thou must save, and Thou alone."

Oh, the joy of this assurance,
God and sinners reconciled;
Free forgiveness through the merits
Of the Sinless Crucified:
"In my hand no price I bring,
Simply to Thy cross I cling."

Evermore be Christ my glory,
As I tread the narrow way;
Pressing on through doubt and danger
To the bright and perfect Day:
"Rock of Ages, cleft for me,
Let me hide myself in Thee."

ZION.

"By the rivers of Babylon, there we sat down, yea, we wept, when we remembered Zion. We hanged our harps upon the willows in the midst thereof." — Ps. cxxxvii.

SORROWING souls, who loved so well
 The Zion of our God below;
 Thy harps, when on the willows hung,
  As their sad music ceased to flow,
Breathed but the prelude to the strains
 In dire distress, her tribes have sung,
Whilst with undying love they still
 To her dishonored altars clung.

One day, her bulwarks firm and strong,
 Defiance to the foe has hurled;
The next has seen that foe advance
 Before her tattered banners furled:
No, never furled, nor stricken down,
 But over length'ning vale and hill
The watchman's echoing shout was heard —
 "The Lord of hosts shall triumph still."

Dear heritage, my soul adores,
    Jerusalem, so fair and free!
What clearer light in coming time
    Is yet to be revealed to me?
What greater victories of the cross,
    What powers of darkness overthrown,
Ere the redeemed of every clime
    Shall Jesus, King, Immanuel, own?

DEDICATORY HYMN.

GREAT King in Zion! when of old
    Thy people came to worship Thee,
And prophets to the world foretold
    Thy name should spread from sea to sea, —

How glowed Thine altars, King of Kings,
    With precious stones and burnished gold!
What incense rose, while cherub wings
    Swept over the anointed fold!

What awful majesty unveiled
    Itself before Thy people there!
What praises rang when Israel hailed
    Those consecrated shrines of prayer!

But when the veil was rent in twain,
    A costlier gift than Israel knew
Was on her smoking altars slain,
    As priest and prophet thence withdrew.

Lord, who are we that we should dare
  To build a house for Thee to-day,
If the Atonement offered there
  We might not on its altars lay?

We veil our faces as we bow,
  And feel Thy sacred presence near;
Accept our humble offering now,
  And dwell, Jehovah, with us here.

NEAR TO PORT.

A venerable man who had been a mariner in his early life, and in old age had experienced much domestic bereavement, on being borne from the sanctuary, a smitten paralytic, whispered, "NEAR TO PORT," and died.

N aged man by sorrow bowed,
Looked on a sky without a cloud,
And hailed, as from his bed he rose,
Another day of pure repose.
The echoes of the Sabbath bell
Upon his chastened spirit fell.
He trod with reverential air
The consecrated aisles of prayer,
And felt a presence from above,
Descending as the Heavenly Dove.
No place to him could be more sweet
Than sitting at his Master's feet;
For foretastes wonderful were given
Of the sabbatic rest of heaven,
And his heart cried, "Dear Lord, how long
Ere I may sing the conqueror's song?"

The prayer had but escaped his breast,
When visions of his longed-for rest
Came to him with o'erpowering might,
And thrilled him with excess of light.
He felt the mortal man give way,
The spirit loosened from its clay,
And cried again, "Dear Lord, is this
The dawning of immortal bliss?"
And, as the pearly gates swung wide,
"NEAR TO THE PORT," he breathed, and died.

Near to the Port! O mariner,
Thy message does my spirit stir,
As pressing on through doubts and fears,
I fain would know what round of years
Before me lies, ere toil shall cease,
And conflict end in perfect peace, —
Ere my worn feet shall surely press
The temples of His Holiness, —
Ere, treacherous seas and perils past,
I anchor safe in Port at last.

MEMORIAL.

MEMORIES of the past
Come like the shadows o'er the landscape cast :
Yet why, O faithless heart, shouldst thou repine?
There could not be a shadow, did not the sun
   still shine.

THE GREAT MYSTERY.

THE mystery of mysteries !
  So far and yet so near,
 Is the land of the Immortals,
  To our earthly dwelling here !
So wide, and yet so narrow,
  Is the stream which flows between
The present and the future,
  The seen and the unseen !

THE SMITTEN PRESIDENT.[1]

O ! sea-breeze on the Jersey shore,
Borne fresh the wild Atlantic o'er !
A hero waiteth on the strand,
The prostrate chieftain of our land.
His chariot on the swift winds flew,
So much he longed to be with you.
More than two summer moons ago
The assassin's bullet laid him low ;
And, through long days and nights of pain,
He sought the mastery to gain
O'er Death, whose sternly upraised dart
Well-nigh had pierced his manly heart.

'T is life or death : all human aid
To stay the foe has been arrayed ;
But earnest hearts that never quail,
That scarce dare hope yet would not fail,

[1] James A. Garfield.

Prop up the wasting victim still, —
O master of the mighty will !
Good cheer to-day ! Brave heart, good cheer !
Hope dawns upon thy pathway here.

Fan him to sleep, O ocean breeze !
Sing to him lullabies, whispering trees !
Temper thy rays, O fervid sun !
For th' race his feet have yet to run ;
Light up his pathway, harvest moon !
Grant him, O health ! the longed-for boon ;
Nurse him, kind hearts on the Jersey shore,
Till his dread conflict with death is o'er !

September 10, 1881.

THE LAST MAN AT HIS GUNS.

WELL done! and more thou couldst not do,
    Brave scion of the Pilgrim stock!
When death's defiant missiles flew,
    And warriors quailed before the shock,
And Gettysburg ran red with blood,
    And fiercer frowned the angry sky,
Unawed thy spirit met its doom,
    Daring to conquer and to die.

What though thy comrades fell in heaps,
    As the great wave of battle rolled?
And strong men trembled as the foe
    Swept on with fury uncontrolled?
Had not thy heart its fealty sworn
    To the old flag whate'er the cost?
And from that foe thou wouldst not turn,
    Though all but thy dear life were lost.

Oh, when Columbia gathers up
  Her jewels from that dreadful strife,
And weaves her fairest garlands round
  The forms once radiant with life, —
In her long line of honored dead
  High on the roll thy name will stand,
The hero who sublimely died,
  For Freedom and his native land.

ALONZO H. CUSHING, Captain of Company A, 4th Regiment of U. S. Artillery, killed at the battle of Gettysburg, was literally the last man at his guns. He was born in Wisconsin, January 19, 1841, and was descended on both sides from the Puritans of Massachusetts. At the age of sixteen he entered the U. S. Military Academy at West Point, and graduated with honor in June, 1861. He was commissioned soon after as First Lieutenant of Artillery.

When General McClellan took command of the Army of the Potomac, Lieutenant Cushing accepted the position of Chief of Ordnance, with the rank of Captain, on General Sumner's staff. He was recommended for two brevets for his gallantry during the Peninsula campaign.

February, 1863, he assumed command of Company A, 4th Regiment of U. S. Artillery. The battery took a highly creditable part in the battle of Chancellorsville, but it remained for the terrible struggle of Gettysburg to call out the heroism of his nature, and stamp him, in the language of General Hancock, "the bravest man I ever saw."

His battery was posted on the left slope of Cemetery Hill, and was in continuous action for two days. The Commander of the Artillery advised him to fall back, fearing his guns would be lost. He answered. "Let the battery go: we'll go with it."

He was twice wounded, and was implored to leave the field, but refused to desert his post, and continued by the side of his *last gun*, hurling the advancing foe back with a final discharge as they reached the very muzzle of his piece. thereby enabling the infantry to crown the repulse with decisive victory. At this moment a musket-ball struck him. wounding him mortally. He sank to the ground, but refused to be removed from the field, signifying his desire to remain and die with his battery.

At the time of his death. Captain Cushing was twenty-two years of age. In person he was fully six feet high, handsomely and powerfully built. with prominent. clear blue eyes and light brown hair.

His remains were interred, with military honors, at West Point, on Sunday, the 12th day of July, 1863.

The services rendered by the Cushing brothers in conflicts with the Indians and in the Civil War have not been surpassed by any family in the United States.

MILTON B. CUSHING,
Paymaster in U. S. Navy. died 1887.
HOWARD CUSHING, LIEUT. 3RD U. S. CAVALRY,
Killed by Indians in Arizona.

Alonzo H. Cushing,
Killed at Gettysburg, July 3rd, 1863.
William B. Cushing, Lieutenant,
Commander U. S. Navy, and hero of the Albemarle,
died 1874.

Their mother, Mary B. Smith Cushing, was descended from Samuel Bass, who married Ruth Alden, daughter of John and Priscilla Alden, of Pilgrim memory. She was a lady of rare force and beauty of character, and died, much respected, in 1891, aged eighty-three years; having survived her sons, who so honored her in the service they rendered their country in times of trial and adversity.

BURIAL OF MRS. JUDSON.

SARAH BOARDMAN JUDSON was the second wife of Adoniram Judson, the distinguished missionary to India. She was returning home after an absence of twenty years, when she died near the Island of St. Helena, where she was buried September 15, 1845.

MOURNFULLY, tenderly,
Bear onward the dead;
Where the warrior has lain,
Let the Christian be laid;
No place more befitting,
O Rock of the sea!
Never such treasure
Was hidden in thee!

Mournfully, tenderly,
Solemn and slow;
Tears are bedewing
The path as ye go —
Kindred and strangers
Are mourners to-day,
Gently, so gently,
Oh, bear her away!

Mournfully, tenderly,
   Gaze on that brow,
Beautiful is it,
   In quietude now ;
One look, and then settle
   The loved to her rest,
The ocean beneath her,
   The turf on her breast.

So ye have buried her,—
   Up and depart
To life and to duty,
   With undismayed heart ;
Fear not, for the love
   Of the stranger will keep
The casket that lies
   In the Rock of the deep.

Peace ! peace to thy bosom,
   Thou servant of God !
The vale thou art treading
   Thou hast before trod :
Precious dust thou hast laid
   By the Hopia tree,
And treasure as precious
   In the Rock of the sea !

HENRY MORTON DEXTER.

 COULD not know when last we met
His sun of life so soon would set;
Yet he appeared to me as one
Who felt his earthly race was run;
A reaper gathering his sheaves
As fell the brown October leaves;
A traveller at the close of day,
With shadows length'ning on his way,
Waiting a few to-morrows more,
Till Time and trial all were o'er.

What though the once elastic limb
And strong right arm were failing him?
I thought he never fairer seemed;
His mild eyes never kindlier beamed;
It was that charm which comes with age,
The beauty of the saint and sage;
The spirit, loosened from its clay,
E'en then was on its upward way;

I followed him with love more strong,
As quietly he moved along,
And could not fonder glances cast
Had I been sure they were the last.

And now, as cometh day by day,
I linger on this well-worn way;
Amid the tread of busy feet
We nevermore as old friends meet;
And yet, and yet, he's with me still,
A bearer ever of good will;
All that in life made him most dear
Remains a benediction here:
I feel the pressure of his hand,
That touch the heart can understand,
And fain would lift, O mystery,
The veil between himself and me!

THE HARVEST OF DEATH.

DEATH has been busy through the waning year.
What time that Spring awoke, and jocund shook
Her virgin tresses in the sun, and June,
Fragrant with roses, benedictions breathed,
The Messenger that all men fear came not
As now he hovereth round our pathway.
'Twas when the branches drooped, and on the vines
The purpling grapes hung low, and from the fields
The reapers shouted to the harvest-home,
Thy fearful triumphs multiplied, O Death!
Not faster ran the sands of the old year
Than fell in heaps on every side the slain.
They who had walked as heroes on the earth;
He[1] of the noble mien, whose princely gifts,
Soft as the dews on Hermon, blessed alike
The Old World and the New; the weak and strong,

[1] George Peabody.

All in their turn, were gathered as his trophies.
Yet was his task unfinished. Lo, one more,[1]
A peerless man, lofty in place and power,
In wisdom great, in action strong and bold,
A statesman honored, pure, and undefiled,
His temples girded with the fresh-formed wreath
A grateful nation placed upon his brow —
In manhood's prime, bowed down his head and died!
And then in bitterness we cried, "Enough!
Sheathe now thy sword, thou Slayer of the world!"

Then through the land the merry Christmas chimes,
"Peace and good-will to men," rang out, as erst,
To weary, heavy-laden spirits, came
Tidings of joy upon Judean plains;
Yet, while through opening clouds the sun shone forth,
One arrow more sped from the Archer's bow,
And pierced thy heart,[2] guide of my early days,
My pastor, friend; and, 'mid our blinding tears,
We laid thee, oh, how weary! down to rest.

So we pass on. To-morrow's sun will bring
The dawning of another year, and men

---

[1] Edwin M. Stanton.   [2] Baron Stow.

Will warmly greet their fellows with a smile,
And wish them many blessings on their way;
And robust youth, strong for the race of life,
Will castles build in air, and earnest men
Will plan great enterprises, knowing not
That death is on their track, and fall they must,
As they have fallen whom we mourn to-day.

How greatly wise are they who gather up,
From the sure Word of the Almighty, strength
To meet that hour which cometh unto all!

December 31, 1869.

SAMUEL LUNT CALDWELL.

MORE than I knew passed on with thee,
  Thou who hast crossed the unknown sea !
  And daily greater grows our loss,
Thou honored servant of the Cross.

Thy manly presence, quiet air,
That ever spoke of culture rare,
Thy catholicity and truth,
As beautiful in age as youth,
All leave a void which naught can fill,
As, lonelier adown the hill
I wait, and watch the sun's decline,
Foreshadowing in its setting mine.

Brave, generous soul ! My early friend,
This surely cannot be the end
Of friendship steadfast to the last, —
'T is but th' expanding of its past
To larger fellowship and love,
In the perfected life above.

Dear brother! resting on thy sheaves,
As fall the brown autumnal leaves,
It was a fitting time to die,
With withered leaf and flower to lie,
When promise came o'er vale and hill,
"The earth shall bud and blossom still,"
And Hope breathed her assuring strain,
"The dead in Christ shall live again."

THE MISSIONARY'S BRIDE.

16

WE may not, all alone and unbefriended,
　The mission given us to do fulfil;
The heart yearns ever, till its task be ended,
　For loving words of courage and good-will.

THE MISSIONARY'S BRIDE.

AN INCIDENT IN THE LIFE OF THE REV. ADONIRAM JUDSON.

Dr. Judson was three times married. His first wife was Ann Hazeltine, one of that band of pioneer missionaries who left this country for India in 1812. She was a woman of wonderful energy and fortitude, and sustained, as few could have done, the hands of her husband the first twelve years of his eventful life. His second wife was Sarah Boardman, the widow of George Dana Boardman, his associate in the mission work. She was distinguished for great purity and sweetness of character, and walked by his side eleven years, ministering tenderly to his necessities through much trial and adversity. She died at sea, and was buried at St. Helena, when returning with her husband to their native land in 1845. His third wife was Emily Chubbuck, many years his junior, and somewhat celebrated in literary circles, as a writer under the *nom de plume* of Fanny Forrester. The disparity in their ages, and the fact that she was but little known in the religious world, caused the engagement to be sharply criticised. The wisdom of his choice, however, was soon apparent, and to-day her memory is embalmed in the affections of thousands as one of that illustrious trio of women who shared in the labors and sufferings of this eminent servant of Christ. An incident which occurred in his courtship with this last-named wife forms the subject of this poem.

 YOUNG man in the Pagan world
The banner of the cross unfurled ;
Where Christian foot had seldom trod,
He bore aloft the ark of God.

And published, through contempt and shame,
The Gospel in Jehovah's name.

To his commission so sublime,
He gave the wealth of manhood's prime;
The added strength of later years,
When faith had triumphed over fears;
The seed he scattered fruitage bore,
Which nerved him for new trials more;
Through grace he overcame his foes,
The desert blossomed as the rose;
When, weary with his staff in hand,
He turned toward his native land.
He left beneath the hopia tree
The bride he bore across the sea,
And laid within an ocean grave
Another just as true and brave;
Then trod, his weary wanderings o'er,
An aged man, his native shore.

Oh, never round the hero's brow
Were greener laurels wreathed than now;
Old age embraced, the young man prest
With welcomes warm the honored guest;
His courtly bearing, quiet air,
Bespoke the man of culture rare;

And crowds, charmed by his broken tongue,
Upon his speech delighted hung,
While Zion clasped him to her breast,
And bade her weary servant rest.

But Time a wondrous change had wrought;
And few remained of all he sought;
And tarrying for a while, anew
He longed his mission to pursue;
Yet not alone, — he still must share
The love of gentle woman there;
Some hand must hold till set of sun,
Till his great work of life was done.
So, artless as a child at play,
He wandered up and down the way,
And caught at last a pleasant smile
From one who could his hours beguile,
And acted o'er the lover's part,
And offered to the maid his heart.

Then rumor in an old man's ear
Whispered a tale of doubt and fear;
An Elder, earnest, honest, wise,
The story filled him with surprise!
A pupil of the olden school,
He made the law of Christ his rule;

All plans and projects he abhorred,
Which had not a "Thus saith the Lord."
Should his dear brother, growing gray,
To Cupid's arrows fall a prey?
Should one without a call from God
Tread by his side the paths he trod?
Should gossip sport with Judson's name,
With scandal tarnish his pure fame?
Would the thrice uttered vow, if given,
Meet the approving smile of Heaven?

His duty seemed as clear as day,
And conscience counselled no delay;
So, courage gathering as he went,
With solemn mien and look intent,
He to the village damsel spoke,
And thus to her the matter broke.

" A rumor, child, has come to me
That you will Mrs. Judson be;
Pray tell me, ere that Dr. J.,
Loved of the Lord, passed on this way,
Were you impressed it was God's will
That you should such a station fill, —
That you should to the heathen go,
And lift them from their shame and woe,

And, as His herald, should declare
The tidings of salvation there?
Had you conceived of such a life
Till Judson sought you for his wife?"

" Now, father Peck," the maiden said,
As modestly she bowed her head,
" I trust the Lord is guiding me
To do His will on land or sea ;
You say the Spirit should decide
The question, ' Shall I be his bride? '
I do not know how this may be,
But one thing was revealed to me :
When I was asked for yes or no,
A voice spoke very plainly, ' Go,' —
So plain, my trusting heart spoke out
That simple yes, without a doubt ;
And now I hope that you and all
Will see I 've had a *special* call."

The aged father naught could say
To her reply, but, " Let us pray ; "
And, bowing with the maiden there,
He wrestled with his God in prayer.
He prayed for Zion, that her light
Might pierce the dreadful shades of night :

That the poor Pagan yet might see
The sacrifice on Calvary;
That God would stay his brother's hands,
When toiling in those far-off lands;
That she, his chosen one, might bless
With woman's tenderest caress
The evening of so grand a life,
And be the good man's loving wife.

And so they mated, — you have seen,
When summer dressed the hills in green,
The giant oak, pride of the land,
Alone in simple grandeur stand;
And you have seen the graceful vine
Round the old trunk itself entwine,
And lend to age a charm and grace
The painter's pencil loves to trace.
So she, fair daughter, gentle, true,
Sweet child of genius, fairer grew,
As day by day she fondly flung
Her arms around his neck, and clung
To him, his all, whate'er betide,
The missionary's angel bride.

Morn broke in beauty o'er the bay,
The islands of the harbor lay

Like gems upon a sea of blue;
From out the west a fair wind blew;
A bark, with all her sails unfurled,
Is starting for the Eastern world.
Upon the clear, still morning air
Comes up the voice of praise and prayer;
And tears, how free and fast they fall,
As " Loose the cable," is the call;

While they, the loved, the young bride fair,
And he, with thin and frosty hair,
Wave to us one long, last adieu,—
O memory, how comes back that view!

I see them standing on the deck,
As the brave ship becomes a speck,
Till coast and headland, native shore,
Return their farewell glance no more.

And so I muse ; there is some heart
Ready to bear with us a part
Of burdens that are on us cast,
Some one to love us to the last;
Some hand to smooth life's rugged way
Some smile to cheer us day by day ;
Some angel, with a radiant brow,
Is walking with us even now!

www.ingramcontent.com/pod-product-compliance
Lightning Source LLC
Chambersburg PA
CBHW020804230426
43666CB00007B/848